Advance Praise for *Think Agile*

"Great entrepreneurs, like elite athletes, are both born and coached. In *Think Agile*, Taffy Williams provides some of that coaching, correctly pointing out that today's successful entrepreneurs, while just as determined as their entrepreneurial predecessors, must also be agile, adaptable, and open-minded in a rapidly changing world— just like an elite team athlete who can read the field and make changes in real time. As an entrepreneur, seeking to be an agile thinker, I have learned much from this book."

—JEFF ELIOT MARGOLIS,
FOUNDER AND PRESIDENT, AURORA CAPITAL LLC

"In the 20 years I have known Taffy Williams, I have seen him successfully hone his entrepreneurial skills in several start-up companies. Anyone with an entrepreneurial spirit will appreciate the insights and examples he provides in this book."

—KENNETH BLANK, PH.D.,
SENIOR VICE PRESIDENT, ROWAN UNIVERSITY

"Drawing upon his years of experience as a successful biotechnology innovator, leader, advisor, and investor, Taffy Williams shares impactful 'make-or-break' insights on succeeding as an agile entrepreneur in a dynamic and evolving marketplace."

—AMIR DAN RUBIN, PRESIDENT AND CEO,
STANFORD UNIVERSITY HOSPITAL & CLINICS

"In his book, Taffy Williams describes important ways to enhance agile thinking for new and seasoned entrepreneurs, using examples to show how an agile perspective increases the chances for success while rigid thinking can lead to failure. *Think Agile* will be a useful read for all entrepreneurs."

—FLETCHER L. HARTSELL, JR.,
SENATOR, NORTH CAROLINA GENERAL ASSEMBLY

Think Agile

Think Agile

How Smart Entrepreneurs Adapt in Order to Succeed

Taffy Williams

AMACOM

American Management Association
New York · Atlanta · Brussels · Chicago · Mexico City · San Francisco
Shanghai · Tokyo · Toronto · Washington, D. C.

Bulk discounts available. For details visit:
www.amacombooks.org/go/specialsales
Or contact special sales:
Phone: 800-250-5308
Email: specialsls@amanet.org
View all the AMACOM titles at: www.amacombooks.org
American Management Association: www.amanet.org

This publication is designed to provide accurate and authoritative information in regard to the subject matter covered. It is sold with the understanding that the publisher is not engaged in rendering legal, accounting, or other professional service. If legal advice or other expert assistance is required, the services of a competent professional person should be sought.

Library of Congress Cataloging-in-Publication Data

Williams, Taffy.
  Think agile : how smart entrepreneurs adapt in order to succeed / Taffy Williams.
      pages cm
  Includes bibliographical references and index.
  ISBN-13: 978-0-8144-3430-7 (hardcover)
  ISBN-10: 0-8144-3430-4 (hardcover)
  ISBN-13: 978-0-8144-3431-4 (ebook)
  ISBN-10: 0-8144-3431-2 (ebook)
  1. Entrepreneurship. 2. Organizational change. 3. Organizational effectiveness. I. Title.
  HB615.W554 2015
  658.4'09--dc23

                                                                    2014014692

About AMA
American Management Association (www.amanet.org) is a world leader in talent development, advancing the skills of individuals to drive business success. Our mission is to support the goals of individuals and organizations through a complete range of products and services, including classroom and virtual seminars, webcasts, webinars, podcasts, conferences, corporate and government solutions, business books and research. AMA's approach to improving performance combines experiential learning—learning through doing—with opportunities for ongoing professional growth at every step of one's career journey.

Printing number
10 9 8 7 6 5 4 3 2 1

To Mitzi, Mandy, and especially Pat

Contents

Acknowledgments

Creating a book requires many contributions from many individuals. From figuring out the book concept to writing, editing, design, and marketing, the process is multifaceted. There are several people who made significant contributions to the creation of the finished product and to whom I'd like to express my thanks.

First, Bruce Wexler is experienced in all aspects of this book process. His contributions were such that this book would have never been completed without his expert assistance. It was also Bruce who saw some of my articles and realized that a book would be a logical next step in presenting my ideas for entrepreneurs.

Then comes Bob Nirkind, Senior Acquisitions Editor at AMACOM Books. Bob believed in the concept of this book and gave me the chance to create something to assist in entrepreneurial growth. Bob also edited each chapter with great perspicacity and helped keep the writing process on schedule. Also, I want to express my gratitude to all of Bob's skilled colleagues at AMACOM who have helped with the book's design, promotion, and distribution.

Now let me thank some non-book people. To my parents, Tommy and Lorraine, who taught me that I can accomplish anything if I really wanted to do so. To my wife, Pat, who has always been a voice of reason and support. Many times her suggestions would result in my seeking alternatives to solve problems that would arise. My children, Mitzi and Amanda, have supplied the opportunity to learn how to guide without being overbearing. All of these have contributed to skills I have adopted. They deserve my love and appreciation for all they have given over the years.

I also have some work and academic colleagues I want to acknowledge. I would have never taken on management roles without the help of some of the supervisors I had earlier in my career. They gave me their support and allowed me to have the opportunity to succeed or fail. When failure occurred, they were there to help me turn things around. When successes occurred, they made sure people knew I deserved the credit. It is hard to imagine my achievements if these people had not believed in me. I have told them over the years just how much they helped me and I am most grateful to: R. Bruce Dunlap, who was my adviser in graduate school; Jules Shafer and Irwin Goldstein, who served as advisers in my postdoctoral training; Adam McKee, who gave me my first chance to manage a major program and continued to serve as a mentor over several years.

We are nothing more than the sum of the experiences of what we learned. Much of that comes from trial and error, but a great deal comes from those who took the time to teach and advise when needed. There are so many people who touched my life and helped when I needed it. To each and every one of them, I am most grateful. Thank you.

Introduction

I am an evangelist for entrepreneurial agility because of what I've observed and what I've experienced. Historically, I know the huge contributions small business pioneers have made in every industry, and I know they were able to make these contributions because they thought outside of the box. They adapted quickly to changing environments, and they were open-minded about new approaches and willing to test various options to see what worked. Companies such as Apple, Microsoft, Amgen, and Genzyme began life entrepreneurially and grew into huge organizations because their leaders were brilliant at adapting and adopting, at changing directions on a dime, and at defying conventional wisdom—"wisdom" suggesting that the category has been defined and that a new product can't redefine that category.

The need for agility is greater than ever before, yet obstacles have arisen that can foster a rigid entrepreneurial mindset. I've written this book to help you overcome those obstacles and capitalize on all the opportunities available to small business people who can adjust their businesses and stretch in new directions.

Think Agile will help you develop entrepreneurial agility, but it is also a manifesto of sorts. Entrepreneurs are more important than ever, especially as large corporations have downsized so many people out of jobs. We have a growing pool of highly skilled, experienced professionals who are tired of the corporate world and want to start their own businesses. We also have a growing number of people who are starting out on the entrepreneurial path or are veterans of it. The former may have graduated from entrepreneurial programs in business schools, and the latter have likely started a number of successful (and some not so successful) companies.

You may not realize it, but if you're an entrepreneur, you're responsible for creating 40 percent of the jobs in the United States—and I suspect that this percentage will grow in the coming years. I hope this book will aid in that growth, providing agility-based ideas, inspiration, and tools.

Before going into detail about the book's scope and purpose, I'd like to present my perspective on entrepreneurs and agility, and how I developed it.

AN ENTREPRENEURIAL BIOCHEMIST

I grew up in a small town in North Carolina. My grandparents had come to this country in the early 1900s from what is now called Lebanon. They survived and prospered by creating small businesses. I often heard stories of my grandmother selling newspapers at the age of 12, and both sets of grandparents had their own businesses as adults. As a teen, I spent time working in those family businesses. Despite this genetic predisposition toward entrepreneurship, I gravitated to science and ended up obtaining my Ph.D. in chemistry/biochemistry. Working in the lab, I learned that to do a successful experiment, I needed to be flexible—that if an experimental methodology failed, I would try something else, and then something else again, until I produced the result I wanted. That's the truth behind scientific inquiry.

After receiving my doctorate, I ended up working for the government for the next twelve years, and in the process I managed a number of research facilities and learned how to survive in a bureaucratic environment. A bureaucracy, by definition, is a rigid system, yet I discovered that it was possible to accomplish one's goals by adjusting and modifying the standard operating procedures; that there were ways to cut the red tape and obtain the resources that everyone said were unobtainable. Even then, I saw the value in being flexible.

Moving to the private sector, I discovered that it wasn't just the government that was inflexible in its policies. I worked in various science and technology–related small businesses, and I found that a number of senior executives who had come from big corporations tended to rely exclusively on what had worked in the past for them. Yet, even in this field, to get things done I found it was often necessary to take alternative paths.

In this sector, I moved from vice president/research positions in small pharmaceutical companies to CEO of various entrepreneurial ventures. I founded Colonial Technology Development Company in 2005, and in this role I have provided new and growing medical and technology companies with services related to funding, business strategy, and many other areas. Helping startups and other companies commercialize their technological and scientific innovations has been a primary goal of Colonial, and we've launched a number of successful biotech, software, and pharmaceutical companies.

Most of my entrepreneurial activities are in the fields of science, health, and technology. I've been involved in every aspect of these businesses, from creating business strategies, to raising funds, to launching new products. I've also counseled entrepreneurs in a variety of other fields and have friends and colleagues who have pursued a range of innovative business endeavors. In short, I know what it's like to be an entrepreneur. Over the years, I've learned five valuable lessons that all relate to agility:

1. **Question the status quo.** Time after time, I've seen small companies clinging to strategies and practices that worked in the past but that prevent them from changing as their situations change. I'm not saying that you should always dismiss the status quo, but you should always question it. In our highly volatile world, few things remain viable for long.

2. **Take more than one shot on goal.** When I was working on my Ph.D., I had a mentor who admonished me, when I showed him my flawed experiment results: "Go back and make it work." I was frustrated and thought further effort was hopeless, but I returned to the lab, tried different approaches, and—lo and behold—I found a way to make it work. Entrepreneurs often become frustrated when a new product introduction fails or when they launch a business and expectations aren't met. More often than not, the problem isn't with the product, service, or concept but with the execution. Try again, tweak the process, and see if you can obtain better results.

3. **Banish bureaucracy.** To get things done even in small companies, some structure is required. Bureaucracy, though, is a rigid structure that insists on policies and procedures to govern every business action. Invariably, bureaucracy discourages innovation and encourages conformity. Instead, agility favors participatory decision making and diverse counsel and execution.

4. **Accept failure as the cost of doing business.** Fear of failure causes entrepreneurs to play it safe. When entrepreneurs stop taking risks, they stop being entrepreneurs. I realize that failure hurts and that small business people need to do what they can to limit the damaging effect of failure. At the same time, they need to use it as a learning and motivational device.

5. **Believe you can do anything.** My parents told me that I could do anything if I wanted it bad enough, and I've found that was great advice for both life and work. As soon as entrepreneurs start thinking negatively, they begin falling into safe routines and reactive decision making. If you're going to be an entrepreneur, you need to be optimistic and bold. Certainly you don't want to be unrealistically optimistic, but dreaming big and going after those dreams are what being an entrepreneur is all about.

None of these lessons can be put into practice unless you're positive minded, option oriented, and open to fresh thinking. You won't find many agile pessimists, since rigidity is the result of negative thinking. Entrepreneurs who only consider one option have a fixed perspective on their business. And people who eschew creative ideas are only comfortable with the tried-and-true.

I realize that most entrepreneurs, especially when they're trying to get a business off the ground, become focused on practical considerations—staffing, liquidity, office space, software needs, and so on. I encourage you, however, to keep the five agility lessons in mind even as you're negotiating a lease or trying to find someone who knows how to set up a website. Even as you focus on basic business tasks, resolve to be inquisitive, challenging, and optimistic—all by-products of the five agility lessons.

Let me share a story about two neophyte entrepreneurs who put these lessons into practice.

LEARNING TO LOOSEN UP

Margaret and Jim had spent years working for two different Fortune 500 companies in the same industry, and they had been talking for two years about leaving their companies and starting a business. They both had heard about a new technology with the potential to produce a series of products that would be more durable and of higher quality than what existed on the market. When that technology became available, they decided to license it and start their new company.

At first, Margaret and Jim struggled. When they were corporate executives, they both enjoyed large staffs and budgets, enabling them to achieve their objectives with relative ease and speed. Just as significant, they both knew how to operate within the corporation. They were well aware of the corporate norms, the culture, the policies, and the processes. They were accustomed to working within a closed system; they were acutely aware of the do's and don'ts, the politics, and the legal requirements that HR always reminded them of.

Though they were freed from this system as budding entrepreneurs, Margaret and Jim still retained that corporate mentality. They spent a full day drawing up an organizational chart and figuring out what key positions they needed to fill immediately. They created a budget before they had all the funding they required. They prepared a highly detailed business plan that outlined weekly objectives and listed tactics that needed to be used to achieve them.

It took Margaret and Jim a little while to realize that they were still locked into rigid corporate thinking, and that this thinking didn't translate into entrepreneurship. It especially didn't translate because they heard that a large company was investigating using similar technology to the one they had licensed to create a competitive product line. Out of necessity, Margaret and Jim got rid of their highly structured plans and began improvising.

Recognizing that they had to move quickly and not wait months for all the funding they were pursuing, they began to seek a variety of funding sources. First, they applied for governmental loans and grants. Next, they used their network to find a financially savvy friend to hook them up with an angel investor who would give them a substantial sum of money for a stake in the company. Initially, Jim and Margaret had vowed to go it alone, but they quickly adjusted this thinking, recognizing that the advantages of having the angel investor's money far outweighed having to share ownership with another person.

Similarly, they gave up on their plan to hire key employees at their launch. Without all their funding, this simply wasn't feasible. Again, they adapted to circumstance, dipping into their extensive network of professional contacts to find other ex-corporate people like themselves who had left organizations (voluntarily or because of downsizing) and were willing to provide them with necessary professional services (accounting, information technology, etc.) in exchange for equity compensation.

In addition, they moved away from their initial idea of creating their own manufacturing facility to produce prototype products based on the technology. Lacking the funds, expertise, and time to pursue this in-house strategy, they began knocking on doors of manufacturers with whom they had worked in their corporate careers. Their innovative approach was to create a presentation based on projections of orders if even 25 percent of their prototypes proved successful. They told the manufacturers that if they offered them a discount for work on the prototypes, they would compensate them once a prototype became a profitable product and that they would become a preferred supplier. The third manufacturer they visited agreed to the deal.

Within two years, Margaret and Jim had turned three prototypes into profitable lines. Three years later, they had four more strong product lines and eventually sold their company to one of their former employers for a huge sum of money. Looking back, Jim and Margaret acknowledged that they had to "loosen up" their attitudes and actions before they could make it in the entrepreneurial world.

FOR ENTREPRENEURS OF ALL TYPES

Like Margaret and Jim, you may be a corporate veteran attempting to start your own business for the first time. Or perhaps you are a young entrepreneur with little or no previous work experience, corporate or small business. Perhaps you have been working in the small business world for a while on a number of entrepreneurial ventures you built.

It doesn't really matter what type of entrepreneur you are or what type of business you're in. You may be running a startup with a few employees or a larger business that employs hundreds of people. You may have partners, or be a sole proprietorship, or have significant funding from a venture capital firm, or be on a shoe-string budget with cash provided by your own savings.

Whatever your situation, you'll find that the theme of this book applies to you. There are no exceptions to the agility rule: If you're an entrepreneur, you need to become more innovative, more willing to test new approaches, better able to consider all your options, and more able to transition to new products, services, policies, and processes.

But what if you're running a successful business? Why should you change anything if the business is growing and profitable? Because sooner or later an event or trend will mandate change. It may be something major, like an unexpected technological breakthrough that renders your product obsolete, or it may be a series of smaller industry trends that cumulatively require you reconfigure your services. No industry is exempt from this mandate. In fields like science and technology, most entrepreneurs have felt the full force of change buffeting their businesses and they know that "adapt or die" is their new motto.

In other fields, change has been less visible. Let's say you run a small chain of hardware stores in a rural part of your state. For years, you've made a consistent profit and the relatively weak competition comes and goes but hasn't had much effect on your business. But in the next two years, you may lose more customers to online hardware stores that can offer better prices and one-day shipping. You may find that a global chain, desperate for more stores, embarks on a rural strategy and opens stores in markets it had once considered too small.

Every entrepreneur can benefit by learning to become more agile, even if that agility doesn't seem mandatory at this moment. Many of you, however, are probably in the exact opposite position: Your head is spinning because of all the unexpected events and emerging trends that require you to adjust and adapt. In this book, I provide you with many suggestions and illustrations of how to adjust and adapt.

WHAT YOU CAN EXPECT

In the following ten chapters, you'll find advice that covers a range of topics, from funding, to time frames, to planning. All the advice is designed to help move you away from the conventional wisdom and the status quo and toward fresh thinking and new business strategies and tactics. I'm not going to tell you that everything you've built and all the techniques you've relied on are outdated—you don't want to throw the baby out with the bathwater. Instead, I hope that I'll encourage you to assess what aspects of your business require an agile mindset and then offer suggestions for putting that mindset to work.

For instance, Chapter 7 focuses on "repurposing"—how you might transition products, services, and even people into new incarnations that might better serve a changing business. I offer examples of other companies that have used repurposing strategies successfully, as well as tips for doing so yourself. I tell you about how companies repurposed basic weather forecasting services in innovative and profitable ways, as well as how entrepreneurs retrained themselves and others so their skills were more relevant to a changing marketplace.

I've culled examples from a variety of sources to show you how to use agility approaches successfully; I've also included some cautionary tales of what happens when entrepreneurs are inflexible. Some of these examples are from my own entrepreneurial experiences; others are stories that have been told to me by other small business owners; and some are a result of research. In certain instances, I've used the real names of entrepreneurs and their companies, and sometimes I've changed the names or provided composites when the situations were sensitive.

At the end of each chapter is a section titled "Putting Concepts into Action," which is designed to help you think about agility-focused ideas that were presented in the chapter and apply them to your business. The combination of these prescriptive elements and the suggestions and stories that come earlier should help you navigate your enterprise through a rapidly changing, obstacle-strewn environment that demands agility.

Let's start by looking at that environment and how various trends and events are causing agility to become a skill that no entrepreneur can do without.

PART I

Understanding What You Need to Know Before Adopting an Agile Workstyle

Why should you be more flexible in your attitude and actions?

What are the advantages of an agile mindset?

Where are you on the agility continuum?

The book's first three chapters address each of these questions. I examine why current trends and events compel entrepreneurs to be more open-minded and option-oriented in their approach to their businesses; what benefits accrue to small business owners who make the effort to become more agile; and where you currently are in terms of your agility, based on assessment tools I've developed.

Once you've gained this knowledge, you'll be motivated and prepared to incorporate the entrepreneurial agility tools in the book's next section.

CHAPTER 1

Agility in Turbulent Times

In the past, most successful entrepreneurs possessed a single-minded focus that served them well. Sometimes obstinate and other times obsessive, they drove toward their goals with unwavering commitment. This approach to business—effective in a time of relatively slow change, moderate complexity, and more local than global competition—helped them overcome obstacles and seize opportunities.

While entrepreneurs still benefit from being driven and single-minded, such a mindset can also be a major handicap in our current environment of great volatility and unpredictability. Technological breakthroughs, economic shifts, and other changes occur seemingly every week. There's the adage *Man plans, God laughs*. Substitute *entrepreneur* for *man* and you understand why it's no longer possible for entrepreneurs to lock unwaveringly onto a product, a marketing approach, a business plan, a funding mindset.

Agility is essential for entrepreneurial success. I'll share two stories that demonstrate why this is so.

Though Steven Jobs was an extraordinary and unique business pioneer, he was also a classic entrepreneur in many senses. Early on, he was obsessed with creating the best possible personal computer, and his drive resulted in some remarkable products. But when he returned to Apple after years of exile, he recognized that things had changed. Plenty of people were still buying personal computers, but the market had topped out. He noticed the emerging mobile computing consumer segment, though, and was able to shift his thinking—and the direction of the company—to serve this market (among others). Jobs's flexibility enabled Apple to dominate the space for several years.

Arsen Avakian founded Argo Tea, a retail tea seller, in 2003 and now is the head of a 27-store chain with $20 million in revenue. Initially, Avakian's vision was to make Argo stores the tea equivalent of Starbucks. This hugely ambitious vision, however, did not fit with changing market and economic realities. It also didn't jibe with Starbuck's acquisition of tea retailer Teavana and the coffee company's plan to open tea bars. So instead of trying to become a giant in the industry or do battle with one, Avakian shifted gears. In a September 9, 2013, article in the *Chicago Tribune*, he was quoted as saying that Argo wanted to be the "Apple of tea . . . where you will fall in love with the brand." To that end, Argo has started a bottled-tea business in addition to their retail establishments.

Making these shifts sounds easier on paper than it is in reality. Entrepreneurs often fall in love with their business ideas, their visions for a business, and their theory of how to make their companies successful. To let go of something they love and believe in is difficult; to change it in any way seems disloyal, fickle, and even weak.

Yet letting go requires strength; it's an acknowledgment of a new reality for an entrepreneur. Agility facilitates movement from the tried-and-true past to the changing present.

NOTHING STAYS THE SAME FOR LONG

It's not just that the pace of change has been accelerating, but the types of changes are expanding as well. From the economy to technology to the global marketplace, everything is evolving at a fast clip. More than that, many of these changes aren't predictable. Mobile technology, big data analytics, and social media may seem as if we should have seen them coming, but in fact only hindsight makes it appear that way. Ten years ago, when people used cell phones for traditional phone-to-phone communication, few would have predicted the widespread use of smart phones in ways that make phone conversations a secondary or tertiary function. And until the economic downturn of 2008, the majority of small businesses that required financing sought loans. Who could have predicted that these loans would become almost impossible for many startups to obtain?

In the face of these rapid and widespread changes, entrepreneurs have no choice but to be flexible. If entrepreneurs are unable to shift direction and find new sources of funding, or if they can't reformulate their products when a Chinese company brings out a similar one at half the price, they're out of luck. But before we look at what agility means and how it translates into specific business behaviors, let's review some of the types of changes that make agility imperative:

➤ **Funding.** It's not just that banks have tightened their purse strings, but that venture capital firms have diminished in number; and those that remain are more selective about who they fund. We've seen the rise of angel investors—wealthy individuals or groups who fund ventures in exchange for a share of ownership. We've also witnessed the rise of what I refer to as "startups for sale"—cash-strapped entrepreneurs who launch companies on a shoestring with the hope of becoming acquired by a large company. In this way, they gain the finances and other resources necessary to grow their idea into a profitable enterprise; "startups for sale" has become the dream goal of many entrepreneurial Internet companies. And then there's the crowdfunding movement—people who use the Internet to launch their ideas for new businesses and attract financial backing from individuals who see potential in that idea; Kickstarter is the most well-known example. We'll focus on funding options that have arisen in recent years in Chapter 5, but as this brief description indicates, the environment is completely different from how it was as little as ten years ago.

➢ **Technological.** New technologies impact entrepreneurs in every field in countless ways, and they require all types of adaptations. On the most basic level, technological innovations have caused entrepreneurs to change the way they conduct daily business. For instance, Texas Instruments introduced handheld calculators around 1967 and IBM introduced its first personal computer around 1981. In 1973, a scientist working for Motorola successfully made the first portable handset, and by 1987, over 1 million cell phones were in use in the United States. These devices are now part of our daily existence while the older technologies are phasing out. In the 1990s, the fax was the dominant mode of communication in business. Today, it is quickly going the way of the electric typewriter, as email and other Internet forms of communication have become dominant.

The social media demand that entrepreneurs rethink customer relationships; and information technology necessitates that competitors and potential competitors know about your product breakthrough almost immediately after you achieve it. Virtual meetings across continents routinely take place on Skype and other sites. New technologies are being introduced every day, and today's smart phone will be tomorrow's fax machine. Entrepreneurs who aren't able to adjust their businesses to capitalize on these technological changes will be left behind.

➤ **Regulatory.** The EPA, FDA, USDA, and SEC are just some U.S. agencies that have been active in altering their regulations in recent years—and aggressively pursuing those who fail to comply. Any small business that has grappled with the SEC regarding 2002's Sarbanes-Oxley legislation is well aware of how regulatory changes require all sorts of new policies and procedures. Many times, agility is required just in terms of time and resources allocated to respond to those changes. In other instances, entrepreneurs may need to make major shifts in their business operations. New environmental regulations, especially, can create all sorts of issues for small companies: the material you've been planning to use to manufacture your product has just been ruled an environmental hazard, the FDA decides to create new nutrition regulations, or the Department of Energy places greater restrictions on nuclear energy creation and use.

➤ **Market-by-Market.** Entire industries are being transformed through global, virtual, and other means. In the medical field, increased scrutiny by insurers is cutting into medical business revenues. The ability to reduce hospital re-admission rates and the shift toward personalized medicine are causing healthcare professionals to alter the way they do business. Small medical practices have aligned with other groups to create larger medical practices in order to have greater clout with insurers. In other fields ranging from agribusiness to software to beverages to retailing, transformations are also taking place. While big corporations in these fields are affected, the entrepreneurs often are the ones who must be the most agile. Big companies have the size and resources to change more slowly and still survive; smaller entrepreneurs must adapt or perish.

➤ **Competition.** Until relatively recently, some entrepreneurs could occupy a market niche and expect minimal or at most moderate competition. Today, competition has heated up to the point that this is no longer possible. In a world where everyone is in global competition and technology makes it much easier for companies to knock off products, services, and unique selling propositions, entrepreneurs must be nimble enough to fend off competitors. This may mean coming up with a new pricing strategy, redesigning your packaging, changing product formulations, or myriad other responses.

Consider a small, entrepreneurial pharmaceutical company that is developing a new cancer drug. They're planning on investing $50 million in its development and are testing the drug with patients who have not been helped by other therapies. They're tremendously excited by initial results—the drug seems to produce a 24 percent improvement in survival rates—and the company begins working toward FDA approval. Then, news arrives that an Australian pharmaceutical company has gained approval for a similar product. It may be that this competitor's new product makes it impossible to continue development. More likely, however, is that this competitor's success simply means that adjustments must be made. It could be that the Australian company's product will open up a new market, and there's a strategy to piggyback on their initial efforts. It may be that there's the possibility of a merger. It may be that the entrepreneur's product will deliver superior results during testing. The entrepreneur needs to be open to and assess all possibilities and then adjust the development strategy accordingly.

SURPRISES AND COMPLEXITY

It's not just the pace and variety of change that requires entrepreneurial agility. It's that all the changes create a series of surprises and complex situations for entrepreneurs that can frustrate and defeat those who lack flexibility. Complexity can mean many things to entrepreneurs—ten global competitors instead of three local ones; decisions with no right answer; an overwhelming amount of data to sift through; partnering with a competitor; the constant and costly threat of legal actions in a litigious society. Traditional entrepreneurs try to bull their way past the complexity and surprises, and attempt to keep things simple. This hard-charging approach doesn't work nearly as well as it once did. The late Alvin Eicoff, an old-school entrepreneur, founded an advertising agency in the 1950s that made late-night television commercials for products like slicers-and-dicers and 25-piece tool sets. He produced hard-selling direct-response commercials that were enormously effective in generating sales but lacked good production values—they looked cheap and they sold cheap products.

By the 1980s, however, the advertisement environment changed, owing to mergers and acquisitions that significantly reduced the number of firms and created fewer, much larger firms. In addition, cable TV and networks came on line capturing significant market share. Alvin, an industrious and aggressive entrepreneur, recognized that for his agency to survive, it needed to evolve. For that reason, he named a new CEO and sold the agency to Ogilvy & Mather. Soon, the agency was creating direct-response commercials for Fortune 500 companies that valued the advertising tactic's accountability. Many in the industry were surprised that large, image-conscious companies wanted to use this technique. It was a highly complex transition, since the spots for these large companies had to take a different creative approach and media had to be bought differently. The agency's ability to adapt helped it prosper.

In recent years, the Eicoff agency has again adapted to a much more competitive and quick-changing advertising environment. One of the biggest changes in the television direct-response business is that clients no longer want just an 800 number on the screen for a response. They also want a URL so they can drive viewers to websites, and they sometimes want commercials to link viewers to social media. In response to this need for additional contact information, a new, technology-savvy CEO was appointed and the company began bringing in younger, social media–proficient employees to meet this growing need. Once again, the agency's agility helped it grow and remain profitable as competitors' fortunes ebbed.

Surprises and wide variations in the business environment confront entrepreneurs in many types of businesses. Twenty years ago, technology entrepreneurs required a good idea, engineers, and the ability to design software, equipment, and so on—the more sophisticated the design, the better. But then social media and mobile technology changed the game. A tech company can now launch with minimal investment and find employees who work for a year or more for equity and no salary—and no office is needed since they can work from home. To obtain financial backing, they may need to create a prototype or even demonstrate they can generate a decent revenue stream. They may go from rags to riches quickly, as a viral buzz creates so much excitement around the company that they can do a successful IPO or sell their company to a tech giant for a great deal of money. Or they may be blindsided by a company on the other side of the globe that is doing the same thing they're doing—only faster, cheaper, and with better technology.

Consider, too, a more traditional sector. Thirty years ago, the textile industry was a highly regimented business in which quality and marketing were paramount. In New England, North Carolina, and other parts of the United States, the industry flourished and large companies dominated. Then, as manufacturing costs increased, cheap labor available in places like India and China virtually wiped out the textile business in this country. The relatively few U.S. companies that remained in the business had to take actions that would have been unimaginable a decade or two earlier. A September 29, 2013, *New York Times* article described how one Minnesota manufacturer was working significantly under capacity due to loss of skills in cutting and sewing textile products. The firm placed help wanted ads in several languages seeking these skilled workers and eventually had to create training programs to teach the needed skills.

Just about every industry has a story to tell. More to the point, just about every entrepreneur can tell a story about how he or she didn't see a key event unfolding until it was too late or how he was confused and confounded by decisions that seemed relatively simple in the past. Take a look at some of the following unexpected events that have affected entrepreneurs with whom I've worked or who I know about and see if they sound familiar:

➤ A traditional source of funding you've counted on for years suddenly dries up just when you need it most (right before you need the money for a new initiative or venture).

➤ You invite your investors to view the results of your beta test and it fails, despite having worked well up to this point; the technology is tricky and you try and explain this point, but some of the investors you always thought believed in you demand that you return their investment.

➤ A terrific new market opportunity emerges but your resources are severely limited. To take advantage of it you must reduce costs, and the best way to do that quickly is through a staff reduction, but you need your full staff to capitalize on the opportunity.

➤ A young employee files a sexual discrimination lawsuit against the company that you know is completely unjustified. To fight the suit, however, will be costly. You have two 65-year-old employees whom you've been carrying for the last few years and, if they retired, not having their salaries on the books would help with the lawsuit, but you're afraid that if you push them out, they'll file age-discrimination lawsuits.

➤ A Chinese company proposes an alliance with you in which you would provide the product and marketing and they would handle the manufacturing at a much lower cost than your current provider. But the company has been singled out by watchdog groups as operating sweat-shops using underage workers. Its CEO promises they no longer engage in these practices but you can't be sure.

➤ To sustain and grow your company, you need to make long-term infrastructure investments, but your cash is limited and you need to show good returns for the year in order to keep your investors on board.

There are no easy answers to these situations. While you can't plan for the unexpected or find Solomon-like solutions to such dilemmas, you can be agile enough to make the best out of what an unpredictable business environment throws at you.

THE MORE THINGS CHANGE, THE MORE ENTREPRENEURS THRIVE

No doubt, some entrepreneurs long for the good old days when, if you built a better mousetrap, the world would beat a path to your door. I'm not sure how true that adage was in the old days, but today great ideas are only the ante to get you into the game. The good news is that while change, surprises, and complexity make it more challenging for entrepreneurs to succeed and sustain their success, this environment also produces more opportunities than ever before. The key is to possess the agility to take advantage of them.

Consider just a handful of the opportunities that have arisen in recent years:

➤ Online sites that become viable entities much faster than traditional brick-and-mortar businesses

➤ Mobile and computer technologies that allow entrepreneurs to do more with fewer people

➤ Growing receptivity of companies in all corners of the world to partner with small startup organizations

➤ New technology-catalyzed fields that are ripe for entrepreneurial efforts, such as alternative fuels, nanotechnology-based medicine, and analytics

➤ A rapidly growing consulting/coaching sector in a wide variety of fields, as a response to the increasing complexity of doing business globally, virtually, and at great speeds

Despite all these opportunities, one of the most common complaints I hear is that it's no longer possible for a single entrepreneur with brains and creativity to succeed; it's felt that big organizations with large networks have largely destroyed the "ma-and-pa" small businesses, much as Walmart has done to small, local retailers.

In fact, ma-and-pa entrepreneurs probably have better odds of success today than years ago, owing to all the opportunities that have emerged. But they had better be flexible so that they can zig and zag as the environment changes. Consider Sara Blakely, the founder of an undergarments company called Spanx. According to the story on her website, she was working as a sales trainer and a stand-up comedian when she came up with the idea for a type of pantyhose that made women's clothes look better. Starting with a $5,000 investment and little business training or contacts in the retailing industry, she took advantage of all the knowledge available in our electronic age and researched patent and trademark information for her product (which she created herself with a pair of scissors and some pantyhose), as well as hosiery manufacturers in North Carolina.

Blakely was met with one rejection after the next as she visited lawyers and manufacturers, but in response to that rejection she wrote the patent application herself to keep costs down (using what she learned from her research) and consulted a lawyer to help make sure her work would be accepted by the patent office and defensible in the event of litigation. She then drove around the state calling on mill owners and requesting that they make her product. Again, she received a series of rejections until one owner finally decided to take a chance on her product.

Time and again, Sara ran into roadblocks and used her entrepreneurial agility to maneuver around them. Having trouble getting retailers to stock her new product, she flew to Dallas, met with the skeptical buyer for Neiman Marcus, and took her into the ladies room to show her the before-and-after effect of her Spanx pantyhose. The buyer was sold and agreed to take the product. Recently, the media reported that Sara Blakely, who owns 100 percent of her company, is now a billionaire.

What opportunities did Sara Blakely capitalize on that are available to entrepreneurs today? First, the Internet was a tremendously valuable information-gathering tool that helped her discover critical data early on. Second, niche marketers are flourishing at a time when global giants lack the flexibility necessary to hit smaller, growing markets fast. Many huge corporations market pantyhose, but none was sufficiently agile to launch a new product designed to be worn with the latest, form-revealing fashions.

IGNORE THE PAST AT YOUR PERIL

History is a great teacher. As your change timeline probably has shown you, nothing stays the same for long, and the evolution of an industry and a business can be astonishingly fast and transformative. Yet many entrepreneurs underestimate these changes and their impact because they're so busy meeting deadlines, dealing with emergencies, and trying to deal with customers' requirements. The busyness of an entrepreneurial workplace creates the illusion that not much is changing, and that the methods and policies that have always worked will continue to be effective.

And some will. Despite the breakneck pace of change in the twenty-first century, certain entrepreneurial techniques and tactics will be as effective in the future as they have been in the past. I know one entrepreneur who believes with almost religious zeal in hard work. He's convinced his ethnic food product company's success is due to his ability to outwork everyone. And he's constantly coming up with new ways to market his food products, convince a new store chain rep to stock his products or provide them with more and better shelf space, and run promotions that drive customers in droves to the stores to purchase his products. His hard-work mantra is still valid, but the problem is that it's no longer enough. He's facing intense competition from importers who have strong connections with food manufacturers in China, India, and other countries that he lacks. He may have to narrow the range of his ethnic offerings or expand by forging new partnerships.

A brief historical lesson about the economy and technology would serve this hard-working entrepreneur well and demonstrate the value of agility in an age of rapid change. In the last thirty-five years, we've had significant—some might say wild—economic fluctuations. When the economy turned the corner in the early 1980s, the stock market heated up and provided investors with great returns. As interest rates dropped, the market was the best place for money. Then boom-and-bust cycles followed and the market took three major hits: Black Monday (1987), the dot-com bust (2000–2001), and the financial meltdown (2007–2008).

In each of these economic downturns, investors in entrepreneurial enterprises responded with conservative mindsets, and entrepreneurs found it difficult to secure financing as investors cherry-picked the companies with greatest potential, leaving everyone else high and dry. These investors were able to secure very favorable terms or bought the companies at depressed valuations, while many entrepreneurs in the wake of these economic downturns either went out of business or had to sell or merge in order to stay open.

Though we don't know when the next economic downturn will happen, it's likely it will happen sooner rather than later. We live in turbulent times, and the economy is as vulnerable to that turbulence as any other societal component. Therefore, history should teach us that entrepreneurs may need to shift quickly to a different financial strategy—they may need to seek alternative financing (when their investors cut back or pull out), consider a merger, or look to sell rather than being bullheaded and relentlessly optimistic about finding a new investor. Agility here means considering other options, even if they're not ones you originally considered acceptable.

Technology over the last thirty or so years has provided an even more compelling lesson. Around 1985, my company's labs obtained their first desktop computers, which were mostly smart terminals attached to mainframe computers. By 1990, mainframes started to be phased out and desktop computers with enhanced functionality became the norm. The emergence of the World Wide Web made a huge difference for our business, since we were able to access data (limited though it was at the time), and it helped our research efforts greatly. In the 1990s, the Internet took off and our labs capitalized on greater access to data and better computers to analyze a wide range of scientific issues and store massive amounts of data.

In the first decade of the twenty-first century, cell phones became smart phones, computers became even smaller and more powerful, and widespread improvements in electronics created a sameness in products from large companies. Everyone had access to everyone else's innovation and could re-engineer it to offer a similar product. The sameness lasted only so long, at least in the consumer electronics segment, because Steve Jobs redefined how people used their phones and computers. Smart phones allowed Internet access anywhere; photos could be taken and sent immediately while their senders simultaneously listened to music. Computers were miniaturized and enhanced to perform like desktop models while tablets were introduced, rendering computers less essential.

So what does this snapshot of technological evolution tell us? More specifically, what is the lesson for entrepreneurs? It's that you shouldn't fall in love with your technology, no matter how great it is, because sooner rather than later it will be obsolete. That may seem obvious when you read it here, but I've known entrepreneurs to cleave to their technology as if it would remain cutting edge for years and years. Back in the day, there were many entrepreneurs who stayed with mainframes long past their expiration date because they distrusted the desktops. Similarly, some companies have been slow to catch on and become part of the social media/mobile technology trend. Consequently, they haven't benefited from the customer feedback that social media provides. Airlines monitor complaints that arrive via mobile devices while their customers sit on the tarmac, and health-care insurers see complaints or questions arise on various social media and respond before issues get out of hand. The ability to provide feedback and resolve problems quickly prevents the mass bashing that takes place when a single customer is unhappy and others start to relay the message via mobile and social technology.

Entrepreneurs must be aware not only of the new trends in technology but laws and regulations that apply in specific industries, the domestic economy, the global marketplace, and in any other area that impacts their business. They must then translate this awareness to adoption and adaption strategies. This isn't always easy or even inexpensive, but it can save them from being stuck with a mainframe mentality in an age of personal computing—and it might also save their business

PUTTING CONCEPTS INTO ACTION

Awareness is the best first step for developing entrepreneurial agility. By definition and perhaps by necessity, entrepreneurs often are focused on what's happening internally rather than external events. They become so caught up in the quotidian details of starting and running their young businesses that they can't lift their eyes beyond the grindstone. Once they actually look around and become cognizant of all the changes that are taking place, they recognize that they can't continue on a fixed path. Awareness of complexities, surprising trends, and transformative events motivates small business people to think and act differently.

To foster an awareness of the complexities, trends, and events that might motivate you to think and act differently, create a change timeline for your industry and your business. History provides a compelling perspective. For that reason, I'm suggesting you note the key events, trends, and developments that have taken place in your field and in your company during the last thirty to fifty years. Here are some questions that will help you create this timeline:

1. What were the major products and services offered in your sector twenty years ago and what are they today?

2. Who were your main competitors ten years ago, five years, ago, and who are they now?

3. In years past, what (if any) were the global events that affected your business? What are the global trends that have had an impact in recent years?

4. What was the biggest concern of companies in your industry thirty years ago? Fifteen years ago? Today?

5. How has the dominant technology in your field changed over the decades?

6. Over the past ten years, how has the quality of your work environment changed? Can you chart changes on a yearly basis in terms of your stress levels (on a 1 to 10 scale),

crises (number and seriousness of), and workload (overwhelming, heavy, medium, mild, easy)?

7. If you've been in business for a relatively short period of time, can you identify your most significant problem on a month-by-month basis?

Think with a historical perspective in order to create a flexible mindset. For instance, you recognize the necessity of investing in new equipment to ensure that your factory will remain state-of-the-art, but you also need to stay as liquid as possible over the next year because you anticipate some significant short-term expenses. The complexity is short-term versus long-term, and it's caused by an increasingly competitive environment. In the past, you may have been able to get away using your "old" equipment for a longer period of time, and you had fewer short-term costs caused by compliance issues, legal fees, and so on.

Complexities can revolve around situations such as hiring or firing decisions (the right person for the job wants too much money), mergers/acquisitions (should you sell the company to a big corporation and risk losing independence), or outsourcing (should you give up a function you're not good at but at the price of complete control of the function). Create a list of the complex, confusing, and frustrating situations you've faced in the past year, and ask yourself the following questions:

1. Did you respond by making the same decision you always have made, even though you suspect it will no longer be as effective?

2. Did you decide to do nothing, hoping that things will "sort themselves out" while you sit on the fence?

3. Did you rely on your ingenuity to make a good decision?

If you answered yes to this last question, you probably dealt with the situation effectively. Creativity is agility in action. Entrepreneurs who think out of the box when faced with conundrums, paradoxes, dilemmas, and the like are thinking flexibly.

Finally, determine the number of surprises you've encountered in your business recently. Again, make a list of events or situations that caught you off guard. The purpose here is to raise your awareness of how many unexpected developments have impacted your business. By surprises, I'm referring to significant events, not relatively minor ones (such as your assistant deciding to take a leave of absence to be a stay-at-home dad). To help you create your list, here are some common examples of surprises entrepreneurs have encountered in recent years:

- A sudden high turnover rate as your employees leave for better offers
- A surge of new business that requires you to add staff and other resources
- A loss of business when three key clients leave in a matter of months
- A new law or regulation that requires a number of business changes to be in compliance
- A major economic swing has a positive or negative effect on your business
- A strong competitor appears on the scene that you have never heard of or considered a lightweight
- An unanticipated lawsuit is filed against your company
- A larger company makes an acquisition or merger offer
- A technology innovation changes the competitive landscape of your industry

CHAPTER 2

Reaping the Benefits of Agility

Agility isn't just a nice skill for entrepreneurs to possess. It's a crucial attribute with tangible benefits. Being flexible provides significant competitive advantages for small businesses— advantages that companies many times larger may not possess. Agility confers speed, innovation, resiliency, and other benefits that are directly linked to being able to think about a situation in a different way and to move in a new direction.

Just as physical agility can't be achieved without frequent stretching and exercise, entrepreneurial agility requires consistent effort. It means being conscious of the need to think and act in new ways and of stretching one's thinking so that the unanticipated and the fresh are always considered.

You're unlikely to make this effort, however, unless you understand the benefits that will result. Most of us fall into routines at work that cause us to cling to the familiar and comfortable. Being agile will take you into new and unfamiliar territory. Venturing into this territory is worth it, as the following benefits make clear.

PIVOTING TO MAKE EFFECTIVE AND EFFICIENT DECISIONS

Unless you're a scientist, you probably haven't heard of Schrodinger's cat. It's what is known as a "thought experiment," created by Austrian physicist Erwin Schrodinger, and it's related to quantum mechanics. In the experiment, a cat, a flask of poison, and a radioactive source are placed in a sealed box. As soon as an internal monitor detects even the smallest bit of radioactivity, the flask is broken and the poison released, killing the cat. In this setup, Schrodinger presents what is essentially a paradox: the cat can be both alive and dead simultaneously. It's only when the box is broken open that a determination can be made if the cat is alive or dead.

I'm not going to explore the mind-bending quantum mechanics aspects of this experiment, but I suggest you consider it from a decision-making perspective. Risks and uncertainty play critical roles in decision making. Entrepreneurs often face difficult choices, frequently involving conundrums: Should they focus on short-term results or on long-term sustainability, for instance? There is no right answer; each choice carries potential risks and potential gains. Entrepreneurs are like observers of the Schrodinger's cat experiment. They can save the cat by breaking open the box and bring possible harm to themselves (because of exposure to radiation), or they can avoid exposure and not open the box but probably doom the cat. There is risk involved in both scenarios— either to the cat or to the human. There is also uncertainty: who knows if the cat is even alive or can be saved? There is no definite, right choice. You can only rely on your instinct in these difficult situations.

Entrepreneurs face uncertainty and risk in their business decisions; they also often rely on their instinct to make hard choices. Without agility, it is difficult to act on your instinct. With this quality, however, you are better able to employ your instinct and make good choices when the data fail to indicate the right course of action.

Agile entrepreneurs are able to *pivot* when confronted with confusing situations, when risk-taking is required, or when every choice seems a bad one. Pivoting is the actionable benefit of agility. It allows you to change direction on a dime and to take an alternative course of action when more rigid businesses are incapable of doing so. Consider what happens when a rigid entrepreneur faces a Schrodinger's cat decision. For example, it might involve a high degree of financial risk, such as securing a loan for expansion; or it might be a situation rife not only with risk but also with ambiguity—say, confronting a difficult customer who has promised to place larger orders but has failed to do so.

The rigid entrepreneur deals with these situations by:

➤ Doing what he or she has always done

➤ Postponing the decision

➤ Weighing A versus B

The agile entrepreneur makes the choice by:

➤ Considering the alternatives to maintaining the status quo

➤ Acting quickly

➤ Weighing A versus B versus C versus D

Here's an example of an entrepreneur who was able to pivot

when faced with a difficult decision: Anne was recruited to head a small public company, in large part because the company wanted to capitalize on her technology-related knowledge and skills. They were developing what they were sure would be highly marketable products, but then product development and the stock price both entered a relatively flat period. The board hired Anne, hoping her innovative mindset and risk-taking ability would help them revive the company's performance. Anne began studying alternative products, their categories, the competition, and the company's financial resources; and she reached the disturbing conclusion that the products currently under development would be outdated by the time of product launch. This meant the company would never achieve its former glory; at best, it would return a decent profit for a few years before being eclipsed by competitors. Anne informed the board of this and explained that even if they tried to revive their product development strategy, it was doubtful they could raise sufficient capital from investors to fund that revival.

Rather than milk the current technology or refocus the company's resources on the company's other products, Anne presented the board with an alternative: seek and acquire a new, cutting-edge technology and use it to develop a new product. The company had never done anything like this before, and Anne admitted that it carried a degree of risk. She brought in some advisers from the tech community who were optimistic about her plan, and the board gave her the go-ahead. Within a few months, they found and acquired a new technology, developed a product based on it, and reconfigured the company to take advantage of what Anne and her advisers were convinced could be a breakthrough product in its category. Investors agreed, and significant funds were raised to support the product launch. As a result, the company increased in value from $3 million to over $300 million in five years.

Anne's agility allowed the company to achieve what no other business in its industry was doing. She made the decision to set the company in a completely new direction, and she made it with great speed. Pivoting allowed her to break with the past and embark in a new, more timely direction.

CULTIVATING A FLEXIBLE MINDSET TO OVERCOME INDECISION

Entrepreneurs are often risk-takers by nature but, paradoxically, they can also be indecisive in certain situations. When overwhelmed by data or facing multiple options, they may be unable to pull the trigger. Instead of seizing an opportunity and taking action, they may fuss and fret until it's too late. In the late to mid-1990s, Martin was a highly successful commodities trader who was keenly aware of the growth of dot.com companies, as well as the birth of new "support" businesses as the World Wide Web became the Internet. Martin had been skilled at commodities trading because he could make decisions quickly and instinctively; he relied on his experience and his financial acumen to guide his risky buying and selling decisions.

As an investor, though, he was overwhelmed by the technology-related investing options open to him. At one point, a friend told him about a new, small company that designed websites for large organizations. Martin went to its headquarters—a dingy, converted warehouse—and despite its physical appearance was impressed by the technological savvy of the company's top people, as well as their ability to create ergonomic, visually stunning sites. The business required a $500,000 investment, and Martin found himself unable to make the decision as to whether to invest. Bombarded with other tech-related investing opportunities, he analyzed and analyzed, and eventually fell victim to analysis paralysis. Two years after passing on this investment, the company was sold for just under $70 million.

Agility is an antidote to indecision. Cultivating a flexible mind-set helps entrepreneurs choose among multiple options rather than become overwhelmed by them. Though people complain about today's unsettled business environment and its rapid pace of change, one advantage is that it provides entrepreneurs with a much greater variety of choices. New technologies, new markets, and new electronic systems all yield alternatives that didn't exist in the past. The agile entrepreneur is able to consider all these alternatives and choose one from many.

The rigid entrepreneur rationalizes indecision and clings to the status quo, coming up with 101 reasons why it's best to do nothing: the timing is wrong; the reward doesn't justify the risk; the market is changing; the government is considering legislation in the field. All of these reasons may have some validity; I'm not advocating plunging headfirst into any decision, without first some careful analysis and weighing of risks.

But entrepreneurs suffer small deaths when they do nothing. Like sharks, they need to keep moving forward. Even if a choice doesn't work out as anticipated, entrepreneurs learn from it; at times, the bad choices give them information and ideas that make for much better decisions the next time.

OPENING UP A UNIVERSE OF POSSIBILITIES

Many small business leaders are drowning in details. No matter how creative they may be, their daily routine consists of reviewing a barrage of facts, figures, and nitty-gritty issues. They spend an hour talking about upgrading their company coffee service; they're in a two-hour meeting that revolves around a direct report's complaint about a difficult but talented colleague; there's a lunch to straighten out a misunderstanding with a customer, followed by a long, protracted afternoon negotiation with a vendor over pricing.

This is a necessary part of the job, but it can hamper creativity. Rather than opening their minds to a universe of possibilities, some entrepreneurs glimpse only their tiny corner of the world. Agility has the benefit of widening this perspective. More specifically, an agile entrepreneur is like my friend and entrepreneurial maven Ashleigh Palmer, who glimpses innovative products and strategies that others miss. His mind takes in an event or a series of events and translates them into new and highly profitable businesses that few others have envisioned.

For example, nitric oxide is a free radical pollutant gas that reacts rapidly with oxygen and moisture to create toxic by-products. It is readily available from industrial gas companies, which use it to calibrate Environmental Protection Agency monitoring devices. In the early 1990s, Ashleigh was working at an anesthesia subsidiary of a large industrial gas company. University-based research revealed that nitric oxide could treat "blue babies" who suffered from a life-threatening lung problem due to lack of oxygen, a condition that caused their skin to turn blue. An inventor had approached Ashleigh's company to license the technology and help develop the product for treating this life-threatening illness in the intensive-care units of hospitals. Like many nonagile companies, this large, risk-averse company initially resisted the inventor's request for licensing.

Simultaneously, Ashleigh became aware of what this inventor was proposing, as well as the university research behind it, and he recognized the potential medical use of nitric oxide. He convinced the gas company to take an option on the technology. Ashleigh created a great team and developed a plan to capitalize on the opportunity. It was no small task for him to raise the gas company management's awareness and interest, but when Ashleigh's group accomplished this objective, they were able to obtain funding and created a unique business model for this new medical product. Ashleigh's agility was evident throughout the endeavor, but especially in how he developed a novel pricing model that resulted in excellent earnings for what came to be an FDA-approved medical product. Ashleigh's wide-ranging and mutable vision for new companies helped turn a licensed research idea into a $240 million orphan drug pharmaceutical franchise representing 20 percent of the gas company's EBITDA (earnings before interest, taxes, depreciation, and amortization). That franchise was subsequently sold in 2007 to the critical care company Ikaria for $670 million.

Agile entrepreneurs have a remarkable ability to see opportunities that others miss. They ask themselves a lot of "what if" questions: What if we sold our established product to a new market in a new way? What if we shifted our strategy and targeted a small group of customers with more money to spend? What if we reduced our expenses by 2 percent and invested the money in marketing? What if we partnered with a young, upstart company that has skills in search engine optimization and other analytics that we lack?

These agile entrepreneurs generate additional possibilities that sometimes translate into new opportunities. Consider a classic example from the tourism business. Haleakala National Park in Hawaii has an extinct volcano located 10,000 feet above sea level. For years, it was a curiosity visited by relatively few, owing to the difficulty in getting there. Then an entrepreneur asked the question: What if you provided bus rides to the top of the extinct volcano and advertised it as a great way to see fabulous sunrises? Another entrepreneur asked a different question: What if you appealed to a more active market and rented bikes to tourists and emphasized the 26-mile downhill ride post-sunrise? Now there are several profitable companies providing the bikes, buses, and tours.

Dr. Donalee Markus specializes in visual imagery exercises (i.e., puzzles where you must determine the next shape in a sequence) designed to increase brain plasticity. In many cases, people are stumped by the puzzles initially, and to help them get unstuck she provides them with tips such as, "Turn the puzzle sideways and look at it from a different angle." Suddenly, a puzzle that appeared unsolvable begins to make sense.

To create innovative agility, entrepreneurs must do the same, shifting their point of view to consider alternatives. Taking new looks at familiar products, services, and situations can yield fresh insights. But it requires a conscious shifting. Entrepreneurs must ask the what-if questions that help them gain access to creative business options that are hiding in plain sight.

REBOUNDING FROM MISTAKES AND FAILURES

If you don't have a healthy ego, you probably shouldn't be an entrepreneur. The act of starting and running a relatively small business in the twenty-first century requires chutzpah, which is why many entrepreneurs are confident and aggressive as businesspeople. It's not a question of whether the company will stumble but of when and how badly. That said, egos are fragile, and more than one entrepreneur has found him- or herself beset with self-doubt and unwilling to take risks after experiencing failure. Mark, for instance, ran a thriving consulting business that was growing so quickly he knew he needed help. He found a partner who wanted to buy into the business and he possessed complementary skills and resources. Agreeing to a partnership was a difficult decision for Mark, but he took a chance and during the first year, the business flourished. Then, when the economy went south, the business struggled and Mark's partner embezzled money from the company, almost destroying it. Though Mark was able to get the company back on its feet, he became risk-averse and conservative after this experience, and the company never regained its former profitability.

Mark wasn't agile, and as a result of what he termed "my abysmal failure in judgment," he began questioning every decision he made, afraid of committing another error. Agility gives entrepreneurs the resilience to rebound from mistakes. It doesn't make mistakes easier to accept. Agile entrepreneurs beat themselves up for bad decisions just as inflexible businesspeople do, but they have the flexibility to roll with the punches. They make a mistake, they berate themselves, and they move on. I know of a scientist who was asked to join a team working in the budding nuclear magnetic resonance field; this team eventually went on to create the MRI and reaped significant financial rewards. The scientist, though, declined to join the team, deciding that this new field would never produce a viable product. Though he was later devastated by his mistake, he grasped that it was a situational error rather than a fatal character flaw. He learned from what he did wrong—he based his decision on too little information and insufficient analysis—and when the next opportunity came along, he took advantage and profited from it.

Consider what inflexible entrepreneurs do when they make mistakes or experience failure. They:

➤ Become mired in feelings of shame and stupidity.

➤ Feel paralyzed and are unable to take significant business action or assume risk.

➤ Keep their feelings bottled up inside, in part because they are uncomfortable talking about their misstep.

➤ Lose confidence and drive.

➤ Ascribe the mistake or failure to some flaw in their entrepreneurial personality.

Contrast that with how agile entrepreneurs respond. They:

➤ Overcome momentary self-doubt, embarrassment, and anger.

➤ Force themselves to try something new, seize an opportunity, and take another risk soon after their mistake.

➤ Communicate their anger and other feelings to a coach, team, or other advisers.

➤ Become energized by their mistake and are eager to prove themselves by trying something new.

➤ Recognize that the mistake was a result of a variety of situational factors rather than believe they are bad businesspeople.

Agility suggests that entrepreneurs possess the balance and grace to sidestep problems, but sometimes that's not possible. Agile entrepreneurs can get back up quickly when they're knocked down. Being resilient, they dust themselves off and keep moving forward.

ADAPTING TO CHANGING TIMES

Embracing agility means not clinging to the past. Entrepreneurs, especially successful ones, tend to fall in love with their products, their business models, and their styles of operating. They're tremendously proud of the product or service they have created or how they built a company and a culture. Technology entrepreneurs are frequently passionate about the innovative products they've developed, and they have difficulty acknowledging when new innovations have rendered their software or other products obsolete or at least less than cutting edge.

When people consider alternatives regularly, though, they are able to avoid locking into a singular mindset. In our volatile environment, we need to be prepared to adapt to changing circumstances. Consider all the transitions you've faced in recent years, perhaps from:

➤ Sole proprietor to a partnership

➤ An independent company to an acquired one

➤ Selling one product or service to selling multiple ones

➤ Supervising a few people to supervising ten or more

➤ Operating in anonymity to being observed closely by media, competitors, governmental agencies

➤ From operating the business by the seat-of-your-pants to running a company with policies and procedures

➤ Having a miniscule budget to enjoying a much larger one

These transitions aren't easy, and I know entrepreneurs who have failed to make them in spirit, if not in fact. For instance, Tommy started a tiny company that produced an app for a popular mobile phone with two friends from business school. They did it mostly for fun and not because they thought they could make a living at it. After a year, though, the app became enormously popular and suddenly Tommy and his college friends were running a real business. They hired thirty people in a matter of months, and it soon became apparent that the extreme informality was no longer effective—some of the new people weren't showing up on time for work, others failed to take direction seriously. Tommy's two friends insisted that they needed to hire an office manager, create a policy manual, and determine a fair system for compensation and promotions.

Tommy couldn't abide any of it. He told his friend that they had started the company because none of them was interested in working within a corporate bureaucracy, and he reminded them that they had agreed they wanted to create a fun, spontaneous environment. His friends insisted that they could still create a relaxed, noncorporate structure with a minimum of red tape, but that they couldn't continue to run a business in a chaotic, unstructured manner. Tommy refused to compromise or change. His friends bought him out of the business, which tripled in value over the next year.

Adapt to changing circumstances by doing the following:

➤ **Read and learn.** Fresh knowledge catalyzes change. Read about developments in your industry and about management practices and technologies on the horizon. Take classes and workshops. People are often reluctant to change because they lack a sufficient "weight" of information. When you gather the data and ideas that demonstrate the status quo is no longer viable, you're motivated to do something different. When you gather the information before your competitors, you're even more motivated, since it gives you a head start on implementing a more viable product or method.

➤ **Network, network, network.** Networking is a more active form of learning than reading and listening. Go to industry trade conferences, schedule lunches with experts and influencers, attend cocktail parties, and have coffee with people who possess knowledge you lack. Talk and listen, but also exchange information and ideas in dialogues that stimulate your thinking. The active nature of networking forces you to articulate your views and ideas, and in this way you can better examine if they're still relevant. When you express your opinion, someone may challenge it. When you hear someone else's viewpoint, you may be prompted to reassess your own. All of this helps you consider whether making a change is worthwhile.

➤ **Refine strategy and adjust goals.** Learning and talking are necessary initial steps, but you have to do something with what you discover. The key questions to ask are: How did what you learn impact how you're running your business? How did this knowledge affect the objectives you set for the business? Consider whether there's a compelling reason to refine your strategy or adjust your goals. And don't think this annually—think it regularly. The more you juxtapose knowledge acquired with strategy and goals, the easier it will be for you make agile moves to align your business with a changing environment.

CONSIDERING DIVERSE APPROACHES TO FUNDING

Cobbling together different types of financing is often a good strategy for agile entrepreneurs. Admittedly, it's simpler and easier to get money from one source, but times have changed and it may be more feasible to think holistically about this issue. To capitalize on this benefit, therefore, you must consider as many options as possible.

Helaine was a serial entrepreneur. By the time she was 40, she had started three companies, each successful and sold to a larger company at a profit. Helaine had always raised the money she needed for her startups from venture capital firms; she had good connections with these firms and was skilled at presenting her case for investment. Yet as venture capital funds shrank after the economic downturn of 2007–2008, she found it increasingly difficult to obtain the money she needed for her fourth startup.

At first, she did the entrepreneur's equivalent of beating her head against a wall; she kept calling on her venture capital contacts and kept being turned down. After wasting months in this futile endeavor, the reality sank in: she needed to consider other funding options. In years past, she had given these options little thought. There wasn't much point as long as venture capital was available to her.

Over the next few months, Helaine recognized that if she didn't open her mind to other possibilities, she wouldn't be able to obtain funding. Becoming agile didn't happen overnight; it was a series of small, gradual steps. She had heard from a fellow entrepreneur about how he had partnered with a larger company, receiving funding in exchange for five years of exclusive rights to the product under development. This knowledge encouraged her to explore some partnership possibilities, and even though none of them worked out, her efforts in this new direction increased her flexibility.

As often happens, one thing leads to the next. A prospective partner she was talking to told her about an incubator project in her city focusing on high-tech startups; the incubator project connected their companies to angel investors who were willing to invest small but not insignificant monies. Adopting this approach, Helaine was able to obtain half of the financing her new company required. As she was searching for a way to get the rest of the money she needed, she recalled that an older cousin had been badgering her for years to let him invest in one of her startups. She had never taken him seriously in the past, figuring he didn't possess sufficient money to help her. Now, though, Helaine was more open-minded and called him. He agreed to invest, but she was still short of her goal.

Fortunately, Helaine had been doing a lot of reading about small business loans, and her earlier reluctance to apply for one (she had unfairly dismissed them as being better suited for "amateur" entrepreneurs) disappeared as a result of her new agile mindset. She received a loan, and together with the other two types of financing, she had cobbled together the funding sources necessary to get the new business off the ground.

While I'll go into more detail in Chapter 5 about financial alternatives and approaches, here are some alternatives that demonstrate the range of possibilities open to you:

➤ **Friends, family, and former and current business colleagues.** Entrepreneurs often overlook their personal and professional networks for a variety of reasons, such as Helaine's bias against amateur approaches. Yet this group of individuals may possess significant financial resources, and/or can provide you with contacts that can lead to investors. Perhaps even more important, these are people who may trust and believe in you more than individuals who don't know you well, and their faith in your character and abilities may translate into favorable financial terms. Certainly you want to be careful about endangering close personal relationships over financial issues, but if you're clear about the risks and are committed to repaying your investors, you should be okay.

➤ **Crowdfunding.** Kickstarter and similar sites allow you to connect directly online with investors for your project or business. While most people who raise money this way tend to receive smaller rather than larger amounts, it may be a good way to supplement what you've raised elsewhere.

➤ **Small business loans, state and federal grants, military loans, and not-for-profit foundations.** Consider all the possible governmental, trade association, not-for-profit, and other groups that exist to loan small businesses and entrepreneurs money. While some won't be relevant for your particular circumstances, some will, and they are often ignored by the majority of entrepreneurs.

➤ **Vendor lines of credit.** If a vendor wants you to commit to his company exclusively, request a line of credit in return. This arrangement can be a win-win, especially if that line of credit enables you to get your business up and running and turning a profit.

➤ **Angel investors.** These are typically high-net-worth investors who want to get in on the ground floor of a new business. Unlike many venture capital firms that tend to wait until a company has a proven track record before investing their money, angel investors are willing to take more risk by acting quickly and early in the business-building process. They may ask a lot in return, but for some entrepreneurs, the price may be worth it.

INCREASING SPEED OF ACTION THROUGH AGILITY

As most entrepreneurs know, speed kills—the bigger competition. The traditional entrepreneurial advantage in the marketplace is an ability to move faster than larger companies burdened with bureaucratic red tape and other issues that slow them down. Yet entrepreneurs often don't move as fast as they should because they have fixed notions of how they want to test or roll out a product; or how much money they need before they can open their doors, or the number of customer orders committed before they start manufacturing in quantity.

In some instances, these requirements make sense. Too often, though, they are a result of a rigid business mentality. Agility frees entrepreneurs from a long, slow path and opens up shortcuts and time-saving solutions. Let's look at three ways that agility increases speed:

➤ **Faster to Market.** Consider our previous point. An entrepreneur is counting on venture capital to launch his business, but the VC money disappears. He's stuck. Only he isn't—not if he possesses the agility to think outside the venture capital box and consider other funding options. Similarly, agility may mean a willingness to launch before traditional testing is done. Your research and instinct tells you that you have a winner and that the testing will yield no new information, and you follow your gut. The value of getting to market fast in this day and age is enormous. First-mover status confers status and recognition. For entrepreneurs with products under patent, it provides a bigger selling window (the faster the product is introduced, the longer it's protected by the patent). What's more, investors are always impressed by a company that can bring a product or service to market quickly, resulting in more investment dollars.

➤ **Accelerated Manufacturing.** While the manufacturing process must be rigid to ensure quality and avoid errors, it requires a degree of flexibility to move around the typical slowdowns and roadblocks that occur in the process. Plant managers who possess a certain amount of creativity are often able to do "workarounds" when a machine fails or a part isn't available. They subcontract out part of the process; they install a temporary fix to keep the machinery running. Speed in manufacturing reduces overhead and facilitates rapid delivery to customers, two sub-benefits of speed that can mean a lot to a small business.

➤ **Quicker Communication and Responses to Roadblocks and Inertia.** Being agile means being able to compromise when a stalemate occurs, and finding ways to take action rather than take a wait-and-see approach. Agile entrepreneurs don't sit on information or ruminate for days or weeks or months. They find ways to force themselves to take action, even in the face of conflicting opinions and bewildering options.

This last point hits close to home. For years, I've struggled with continuous advice and feedback from advisers, board members, consultants, and others. As much as I appreciate the input, I often find that differences of opinion and contradictory data make me want to do nothing. Isaac Newton's first law of motion is: "An object at rest tends to stay at rest, while an object in motion tends to stay in motion." Entrepreneurs need to be in motion, and the best way to do so is by acting quickly. Agility lubricates entrepreneurial actions because it allows you to move in all sorts of directions—not just the one in your business plan or the one that's fixed in your head. This has been a huge benefit in my business ventures. Just reminding myself that it's better to do something than nothing gets me moving. It also helps to remind me that even if I'm moving in the wrong direction, I possess the agility to shift directions in an instant if I so choose.

PUTTING CONCEPTS INTO ACTION

At the start of this chapter, I underscored the importance of being conscious of agility's benefits, which are what can motivate you to become more agile. As you read through each of the actions and benefits discussed, some may have seemed more relevant to you than others. That's fine. The benefit that resonates strongly with you is going to be the one that addresses an issue you're current-ly struggling with. For instance, if your funding for a new project just fell through, you're going to pay particular attention to "Considering Diverse Approaches to Funding."

It's important that you understand how each action and ben-efit helps counteract the negative thinking and misconceptions that can beset entrepreneurs under stress. These benefits are antidotes to risk-avoidance, ultra-conservative policies, and dan-gerous assumptions that can hamper even the best entrepreneurs going through difficult times.

The following exercise lists each of the benefits covered in the chapter, followed by a list of three common negative thoughts and beliefs that relate to each benefit. Go through the list and make a check mark next to the ones that you've experienced and keep them in mind as you learn how to develop your agility in the fol-lowing chapters.

Pivoting to Make Effective and Efficient Decisions

- ❑ I'm stuck between two different but seemingly equally viable choices.

- ❑ I'm tempted to stay with the status quo even though I suspect it will be less effective in the coming months or years.

- ❑ I'm rationalizing choices that are overly conservative and safe.

Cultivating a Flexible Mindset to Overcome Decision

- ❑ Analysis paralysis: the data is enormous, confusing, and keeping me mired.

❑   Worst-case scenario nightmares: I keep imagining the worst if I make a given choice.

❑   I'm feeling safe and comfortable by avoiding tough choices.

Opening Up a Universe of Possibilities

❑   I'm pursuing moderately effective strategies that fail to provide the breakthroughs and big profits I seek.

❑   I'm struggling with taking the risks that anything bold and creative sometimes requires.

❑   I have fears of being criticized or rejected by board members, colleagues, the media, or customers for doing something out of the ordinary.

Rebounding from Mistakes and Failures

❑   I'm convinced that one failure or mistake will lead to many more.

❑   I'm losing confidence in my ability to introduce a new product or service successfully.

❑   I'm worried that my competitors know more than I do or are better than me because they've been more successful.

Adapting to Changing Times

❑   I'm trying to convince myself that things will return to the way they were and my obsolete strategy will again be relevant.

❑   I'm telling myself that I'm the exception to the rule, that others have to change but I don't (because I have a better product, better services, better strategy).

❑ I'm convinced that change is in the future; I'm fine maintaining the status quo for at least a year.

Considering Diverse Approaches to Funding

❑ I'm willing to rely on one method to finance my ventures, unwilling to depart from a long-used approach.

❑ I'm insisting that a singular method of gaining investors will work as soon as the economy/industry rebounds.

❑ I'm focusing on all the negatives of every untraditional (for me) financing approach.

Increasing Speed of Action through Agility

❑ I'm telling myself that I'm the tortoise and my competitors are hares; I'll get to market after them with a superior product.

❑ I'm certain that speed in manufacturing or delivery or service comes at a high price (mistakes, high costs, cutting corners).

❑ I believe that in volatile and confusing environments, the best approach is to take things slow.

CHAPTER 3

Assessing Your Agility

Most entrepreneurs I know consider themselves to be flexible in their business dealings. Though they might admit to be unyielding in their pursuit of a goal and stubborn in their sticking with a strategy, they'll say things like, "I'm able to drop whatever I'm doing and move quickly if the right deal presents itself" or "I may be obstinate, but if someone convinces me I need to go in a new direction to capitalize on an investment, I'll do it in a heartbeat."

Entrepreneurs like to think of themselves as agile, but they often mistake being agile for being opportunistic. Given a compelling set of circumstances, like the opportunity to make a lot of money, they possess sufficient motivation to try something new or to shift their strategy; they may start out targeting a younger demographic, but as soon as their analytics reveal that a significant percentage of orders are from older customers, they broaden the reach of their advertising. Alternatively, they may identify an interesting technology and proceed to develop it, only to find their path did not fit the intended use of the product—sometimes referred to as a "technology searching for an application." Many times, however, they adhere to a fixed path, and don't recognize that their stubbornness and single-minded drive can hurt their business as easily as help it.

Entrepreneurial agility is crucial. But if you haven't been brutally honest with yourself as to how agile you really are, welcome to the club. Many entrepreneurs lack the time or inclination to examine their own behaviors and analyze which are positive and which are negative. They're so busy with their daily responsibilities and so stressed from them that they make assumptions that might not be correct.

UNCONSCIOUS RELIANCE ON THE TRIED AND TRUE

Most entrepreneurs rely on their strengths in crunch time. Faced with an important opportunity or difficult problem, they turn reflexively to a skill or method that has served them well in the past. In some cases, this is exactly the right thing to do. If you've solved problems by throwing money at them in the past, you're likely to employ this same tactic in the future.

The problem, though, is that this reliance results in a one-dimensional approach. It prevents you from being agile because you're dependent on the one tactic that has worked for you, time and again. In some ways, going away from your strength or tried-and-true method is counterintuitive. Therefore, you need to realize how stuck you are in your rigid modus operandi before you can give yourself other options. This is where self-assessment is so critical, since it makes you conscious of how dependent you are on a single way of doing things.

Rick, a commercial real estate broker with his own firm, heard that a Fortune 500 company planned to build a facility in an area where he did a lot of business. The information was confidential and came from an employee of the Fortune 500 company with whom he was friendly. Rick tried to get in touch with the Fortune 500 CEO, but his phone calls and emails were not returned. Rick, a hard-charging entrepreneur who had succeeded in a highly competitive industry because of his nonstop optimism and aggressiveness, decided to fly to the Fortune 500 company's headquarters; when he arrived, he insisted that the CEO would want to see him. He was right—and he was wrong. The CEO was furious that one of his employees had betrayed a confidence—for a number of reasons, the location of the new facility was supposed to be a secret until it was announced. In no uncertain terms, the CEO told Rick he wouldn't work with him if he were the last real estate broker on earth.

If Rick possessed greater agility, he might have been able to capitalize on his "inside" information. He knew from the start that the CEO prided himself on his ethics and values, and Rick could have been more subtle in his approach. If he had been more low-key, if he had started slowly with an invitation to join him for coffee the next time he was in the area, he might have had more success doing business with the company.

Andrea, like Rick, was an aggressive, never-give-up consultant who facilitated relationships between corporations and universities. Unlike Rick, though, Andrea was constantly asking herself questions about her approach to problems and whether she was getting stuck in a rut. This heightened consciousness served her well when she was contacted by a small university that wanted her to help them create an alliance with a large corporation for scientific research. Andrea knew this was going to be a tough sell. Though the corporation certainly could benefit from a research partnership, it had many larger universities that it might affiliate with. Because Andrea was aware of and analytical about her sales persona, she recognized her instinct to do a hard-charging sell job on the large corporation. She valued this approach, but she also saw that this was a situation that required more finesse than hard sell, that the odds were stacked against the small university, and that she needed to build trust slowly in order to have a chance.

For this reason, Andrea worked much slower than she usually did. She started taking the executive out to lunch and getting to know him—not once during the conversation did she mention that she had been hired by the small university to forge an alliance. Instead, she explained what she did for a living and how she represented many different universities, both large and small. She used follow-up phone calls and emails to communicate how she worked and gradually built trust with this executive. It was only during their third lunch that she broached the subject of the small university and research proposal. The executive was interested but refused to do anything more than meet with a representative of the university. It took Andrea months to make the deal happen, but because she was able to vary her sales pitch, she ended up creating the relationships her client had hoped for. For years she had worked on being more flexible in her sales style— she had not always been an agile salesperson—and her awareness and willing to work to become more flexible paid off.

Both Andrea and Rick are highly competitive, a trait many entrepreneurs share. But what Andrea came to be acutely aware of, and Rick did not, was that an almost neurotic fear of losing can arise from a feeling of hyper-competitiveness, and this fear can create a rigid mindset.

ASSESSING YOUR FEAR OF FAILURE

One of the most common reasons for entrepreneurs to become rigid thinkers and decision makers is that they tell themselves they're being cautious and conservative when, in truth, they're afraid of failing. Few entrepreneurs will admit to a fear of failure. Most define themselves as risk-takers. Yet a paradox is at work: the more successful entrepreneurs are, the more they worry they will fail. It's as if they believe that everything they've achieved can and will be rendered null and void with one misstep.

Less experienced entrepreneurs may be terrified as well of making a mistake or of blowing an opportunity. Not having known success as independent businesspersons, they are convinced that if they don't succeed with this opportunity, there will never be another.

There are times when a fear of failure is justified. Perhaps your business is teetering on the edge financially and you need to be extremely conservative in your expenditures to make it through this rough patch. Or maybe you're negotiating a delicate merger or acquisition and you need everything to run smoothly in order to facilitate the deal.

Whatever form the fear of failure takes, whether you're worried about financial loss or losing out to a competitor, that fear creates a rigid, narrowly focused approach to business. It produces a conservative mindset that is counterproductive to trying anything new or different. Most significantly, it causes many entrepreneurs to adhere to a formula—perhaps a formula that worked for them in the past—and fosters the belief that if they deviate from that formula, they're inviting disaster.

Before assessing whether you are burdened by this fear of failure, consider that the careers of many successful entrepreneurs are marked by failure. In 1990, real estate developer Donald Trump's business almost went under because he had accumulated a huge amount of corporate debt; the company survived only because of a bailout from a coalition of banks. Mail-order entrepreneur Joseph Sugarman, who was a genius at creating copy-rich direct response ads in newspapers and magazines for products like Blublocker sunglasses, often reminded his audiences when he gave talks that he had probably failed more than anyone else in the room. And former Yale professor and cognitive scientist Roger Schank strongly believes in the power of "expectation failure"—how people create windows for learning when they expect one thing and their actions fail to achieve it.

I'm not suggesting you should welcome failure but that you should not fear it; when you understand that it's an acceptable part of many entrepreneurs' careers and that it provides valuable learning, it loses its power and does not create a rigid attitude.

Is your fear of failure holding you back from being agile? Use the following questions to help you make this assessment:

1. Do you tend to blame yourself for everything that goes wrong? Do you beat yourself up when mistakes are made, even if they're not necessarily your fault?

2. Have you ever experienced a traumatic business event, such as bankruptcy, a catastrophic lawsuit, or a product failure?

3. Has your attitude toward risk changed? Do you find yourself increasingly choosing "safe" choices because your mind keeps raising worst-case scenarios?

4. Do you rationalize why you're avoiding risk or unwilling to change tactics? Do you tell yourself that you're responding to the economy, to a downturn in your industry, or to a volatile environment?

If you answered these questions affirmatively, then fear of failure may be causing you to run your business in a highly controlled, programmatic manner. When you beat up on yourself for mistakes or experience a traumatic business event and become increasingly leery of risk, you diminish your ability to do things in new and different ways. And when you begin making excuses for your unwillingness to vary your approach, you may not realize that you've become inflexible for reasons that have little to do with business realities.

DEVELOPING AN AWARENESS OF RIGID AND AGILE TENDENCIES

Recognize that you're probably more flexible in some areas than in others. You may be adaptable when it comes to financial issues like expanding or contracting your budget as situations dictate, but you may find it difficult to vary your management style and delegate authority to direct reports. Few entrepreneurs are completely, naturally agile—or completely, naturally rigid. We all have certain activities or functions where we prefer one style and one style only; we favor short, terse communication and would find it difficult to wine and dine and otherwise "romance" a potential client.

This is perfectly natural, but it hurts entrepreneurs when they aren't aware of their tendencies—in terms of both agility and rigidity. I've identified six areas where agile and rigid tendencies are most likely to surface. Three of the areas involve work styles—how you communicate with people, your posture as a leader (controlling versus delegating), and the office policies you create. One is attitudinal or psychological—how attached you become to aspects of the business. One involves the financial function, and another has to do with your capacity to learn (or your resistance to learning).

This is an eclectic group of categories, but they reflect the wide variety of actions and attitudes where entrepreneurial agility is essential—and where rigidity can set in. Assessing your tendencies in each of these six areas will help you maintain your agility strengths and guard against rigidity vulnerabilities.

Communication

Some entrepreneurs know only one way of getting their points across. For instance, some heads of small businesses are bullies, forever dictating what they want done and never making respectful requests. They use this same style in negotiations with vendors, investors, and others. An inability to adapt a singular communication style to a given individual or new set of circumstances can be devastating to a business. People who possess a high degree of communication agility, on the other hand, are usually able to do the following:

➤ Adjust their style and content depending on who they're speaking to and what they want to get out of the interaction (i.e., an order from a customer versus a settlement with a governmental agency).

➤ Get their point across with force and toughness on some occasions and grace and empathy at other times.

➤ Demand accountability in written and verbal communication but also provide support in those messages when people need it.

Money

When entrepreneurs have fixed numbers in their head and refuse to deviate from them, it's often a sign of inflexibility. For example, they refuse to invest in a burgeoning new market until they reach a certain level of liquidity. Or they decline to bring in a vendor they know will provide a better-quality product because his prices are a bit higher than their current supplier. Or they believe in the principle that they must spend money to make money, and that a business must continue to invest in capital improvements and staff even when it's clear it needs to cut back because of market realities.

Another sign of financial inflexibility is adhering to formulas. For instance, when entrepreneurs seek investors in order to start a company or fund expansion plans or pursue other objectives that require more money than they possess, they may experience what is termed "dilution"—they own less of the company than before they sought outside financing. Some entrepreneurs will set a dilution percentage that they refuse to go below, such as insisting to themselves that they must own 20 percent of the company no matter the circumstances. They fail to factor in the positive trade-off that they now have sufficient cash on hand to accomplish their goals.

Are you agile or inflexible when it comes to money? Here are three behaviors that suggest financial agility:

1. A demonstrated willingness to vary budgets annually based on changes (i.e., new marketplace opportunities, or the need to invest in new technology, or cash shortfalls).

2. The absence of neurotic behavior, such as not spending money like a drunken sailor or hoarding it like a miser, in the three money categories—spending, acquisition, and management.

3. A varied history of actions related to financial situations. These include using different tactics to raise money over time (angel investors, venture capital, bank loans, etc.) or creating budgets that are highly situational rather than formulaic.

Attachment

This factor is more attitudinal than behavioral, but it's a key assessment issue because so many entrepreneurs become emotionally and sometimes irrationally committed to a specific product, service, technology, or business. Entrepreneurs who are inventors, scientists, or even just founders of a business are especially likely to become attached to what they create. This prevents them from changing the technology or replacing an aging product or restructuring the business. They are like someone who is blindly in love and fails to see the flaws developing in the relationship.

Attachment rigidity can be difficult to identify in part because people have trouble separating themselves emotionally and become defensive when anyone suggests that they are too much in love with their products or services. But I ask you to try and remain objective as you consider whether you exhibit either of these signs of inflexibility:

> ➤ An unwillingness to give up on a product or business that is no longer profitable, even when your team and your outside advisers all tell you that it's best to be rid of it.

> ➤ Anger or defensiveness when you're told that you're being stubborn about a company, technology, or business method you love.

Power and Control

Some entrepreneurs are control freaks. Under certain circumstances, this is not necessarily a bad thing. Control freaks ensure that every aspect of a company is running effectively and avoid the mistakes that can stop a startup in its tracks. But businesspeople who over-control struggle to change their management style. When the business is growing, they can't bring themselves to hire the help they require or, if they do hire help, to empower them to make decisions. As the business or the business environment changes, they're unable to recruit or keep talent who possess the knowledge and skills they lack. The need for power and control causes them to run the company only one way.

Luis, for instance, was a brilliant financial professional who created a boutique financial services company that served high-net-worth individuals. During the first year of the firm's operation, the company was able to provide its clients with an average return significantly above the norm—it was a bull market and Luis's aggressive investing philosophy took advantage of it. The firm grew quickly in its first two years and Luis added twenty professionals during this time. But then the bull market turned into a bear market and Luis's aggressive tactics were no longer as effective. Clients were clamoring for alternative investment suggestions, and though Luis recognized the need to provide them, he was trying to have a hand in every decision and simply didn't have the time or the knowledge to do so. He needed to create a more team-oriented approach and to empower each team with decision-making authority on investments; his outside consultant insisted that this was essential. Yet Luis refused. Psychologically, he couldn't relinquish control. As a result, the firm's fortunes took a nosedive and though the firm is still in existence, it's a shadow of its former self.

When entrepreneurs exhibit some of the common symptoms of power and control rigidity, they do the following:

> ➤ Centralize all decision-making authority in the owner/CEO of the company.

> ➤ Micromanage the work of people they respect and trust.

> ➤ Refuse to partner with other companies or provide an outside vendor with any degree of initiative or ability to act innovatively.

Conversely, when entrepreneurs demonstrate agility in the area of power and control, they do the following:

➤ Extend trust to direct reports and teams and give them limited or full authority to make major decisions.

➤ Step back and stop looking over people's shoulders, recognizing the value in letting people learn from their mistakes.

➤ Share power and control both internally and externally, relying on direct reports, consultants, boards, and others to help determine strategy and tactics.

Office Policies

Rigidity in regard to office policies can come in many forms. Some entrepreneurs are old-fashioned and insist that everyone must work from nine to five in an office and are not allowed to work from home. Others are just the opposite and encourage open, unstructured environments but have trouble enforcing rules and policies. I'm not suggesting either work style is right or wrong, but that when you limit yourself to one style, you fail to accommodate changes in society and the workplace.

Do you want to lose out on the talents of a mom who insists she can only work half days in the office because she wants to be able to be home when her kids come home from school? Do you want to forgo the talents of a millennial who doesn't like to get up early and does her best work at night?

You can assess your agility in this area by determining if you:

➤ Adapt workplace policies to the needs of current employees, including flex time, work-at-home options, and job-sharing.

➤ Shift from individual contributor to team work styles when situations require it.

➤ Create policies that foster inclusion and innovation,

soliciting contributions and facilitating decision making for a greater number of employees.

Learning

Every entrepreneur must learn new skills and new subjects to be successful, but some entrepreneurs stop learning prematurely. In some instances, a business owner believes he knows everything there is to know. He's worked in an industry for a while, done a lot of reading about the business, and figures he has gathered all the information and knowledge that is necessary. This might be true in a field that didn't change, but in one where change is constant, this inflexible attitude is a handicap. It is often important to remember that, "We do not know what we do not know." The agile entrepreneur will keep this in mind at all times.

Assessment is crucial in this area because entrepreneurs—especially ones who have achieved some success—are often supremely confident in their abilities and knowledge. I'm not disparaging confident entrepreneurs but simply pointing out that this confidence can be dangerous if not accompanied by learning agility. Someone once said that it's not what you know that counts, it's what you know that you don't know.

To that end, here are some defining traits of learning agility:

➤ A willingness to say you don't know and ask questions to find out

➤ An ability to create a diverse group of employees and advisers who supplement your knowledge

➤ A commitment to developing knowledge continuously (as opposed to gaining one particular piece of knowledge or achieving a goal to master one area)

PUTTING CONCEPTS INTO ACTION

At this point, many of you may be thinking that it makes sense to figure out how agile you are in the various areas just discussed, but thinking about it and doing something about it are two different things. The following questions are designed to help you assess your agility in each of six areas we've covered. After the questions, you'll find some suggestions for how to interpret your answers.

Communication

☐ If you were to characterize the style with which you communicate (what you say and how you say it), what would it be? Are you able to vary this style when situations demand it? Are you absolutely consistent in maintaining this style, even when you suspect it is not working well with a particular person or circumstance?

☐ Can you communicate with both strength and softness; are you able to be tough in some situations, empathetic and supportive in others?

☐ Can you tailor the way you communicate to meet the requirements of a negotiation; are you able to vary your approach in order to achieve win-win outcomes?

Money

☐ Are your financial behaviors extreme? Are you consistently and obsessively frugal in the way you manage finances or do you spend freely?

☐ Do you have one specific way to raise funds for ventures; or are you able to use different tactics depending on variables such as a venture's requirements and the economic environment?

☐ Do you possess a singular financial strategy for running

your business (i.e., marketing budget is crucial, research budget is secondary)? Are you able to adjust this strategy as the company evolves and as circumstances change?

Attachment

☐ Do you tend to cling to ideas, products, and people past the point when most others most likely would have given up on them? Do you rationalize this behavior in terms of your optimism and loyalty?

☐ Do you give serious consideration to alternatives that may be superior to the person, product, or strategy that you're attached to? Are you able to distant yourself enough to analyze alternatives objectively?

Power and Control

☐ How often do you allow direct reports and teams to run important projects without interfering? How often do you delegate decision-making authority to others?

☐ Do you tend to surround yourself with yes men and women? Does it seem as if they are reluctant to disagree with you?

☐ How open are you to criticism? Are you willing to listen to it, reflect upon it, and respond with a different direction if you deem it valid?

Work Style

☐ Are the policies that you set months or even years ago still in place? Have you refused to alter many or any of these policies despite complaints from employees?

☐ Do you provide opportunities for people to work on teams as well as be individual contributors? Are you open to letting people work from home and outside of the traditional nine-to-five workday?

Learning

☐ Are you willing to admit to employees, vendors, investors, and others that you're unsure or that you need help? Do you always act certain and decisive?

☐ Are you constantly struggling with a learning curve? Do you keep current with changes in our industry, ask questions, attend seminars, and actively solicit ideas and information from people who possess expertise you lack?

☐ Do you seek or create stretch assignments for yourself? Are you willing to endure a bit of discomfort in order to try something new or take a reasonable risk?

Reflect on your answers to these questions and then do the following:

1. Create a continuum from 1 (least agile) to 10 (most agile) for each of the six categories. Evaluate your responses to questions based on frequency and intensity: If you respond that you always create stretch assignments for yourself (Learning), that represents high/agile in terms of frequency; if you find yourself angrily defending our policy to surround yourself with people who agree with you (Power and Control), then that scores high/least agile on the intensity scale. Note the area or areas where you have a low agility score. These are the assessed areas that you need to pay attention to.

2. Assess whether fear of failure (or of making a mistake) was the reason you recorded a low-agile score in a given area. Ask yourself if your fear is grounded in reality. If you think it is, state exactly what your fear is and why it prevents you from being agile.

Discuss this fear with people you trust and then assess again whether it's a reasonable fear or an illusory one.

3. Make an effort to maintain awareness of the areas where you're agile and especially the ones where you're not. Sometimes, this awareness is enough to keep you on your toes and help you stretch yourself in circumstances where you'd normally fall into routines and rigid behaviors.

The purpose of asking you to conduct an agility assessment isn't to make you feel deficient as an entrepreneur. I know of very few business owners who are highly agile in all six areas. It also isn't to make you magically agile overnight. The process of gaining flexibility is incremental, and assessment is a good starting point. I'm hoping the knowledge you gain from this exercise will keep you asking questions beyond the ones I've posed; questions like:

➤ Am I willing to stop trying to do everything myself and start involving my team in more significant ways?

➤ Am I so in love with and committed to our technology that I refuse to consider if there are other, better technologies out there?

➤ Am I so focused on making money that I've lost sight of other business goals?

Asking these questions helps entrepreneurs consider alternatives besides the status quo, the routine response, the standard approach. It doesn't mean that you have to choose an alternative every time, but considering them is a good sign that you're becoming more agile.

PART II

Increasing Your Agility Exponentially

Now you're ready to start turning yourself into an entrepreneur who possesses agility. Here and in the following five chapters, I provide you with tactics for becoming more flexible in your thinking and actions. Preparing for surprises, developing financial options, learning how to work with different time frames, repurposing, and overcoming your tendency to revert to a rigid perspective are the five keys, and I offer examples and tips that will help you master all of them.

CHAPTER 4

Planning for the Unexpected, Preparing for the Unpredictable

Volatility ensures that an entrepreneur's best-laid plans will go awry—maybe not today and maybe not tomorrow, but sooner rather than later. As I noted in Chapter 1, we live and work in a time where surprises are commonplace and new trends and technologies seem to emerge out of nowhere. *Expect the unexpected* should be the entrepreneur's motto, and while most smart businesspeople recognize the wisdom in this advice, they also continue to make plans.

The late President Dwight Eisenhower said, "In preparing for battle, I have always found that plans are useless, but planning is indispensable." I suggest that entrepreneurs adopt the same paradoxical philosophy. Value the structure, goals, and time frames you've created, but recognize that you may have to depart from them at a moment's notice.

73

Perhaps the best analogy to use here is that of planning a long automobile trip across the country. You chart the route on the map that seems to get you there in the shortest possible time or one that allows you the luxury of stopping at specific locations along the way. You figure out that you can get from point A to point B in eight hours, point B to point C in six hours, and so on. But once you're actually on the road, things change. You encounter bad weather. Your car breaks down. You decide you want to make a detour. So you make adjustments. You go south to avoid bad weather. You're forced to spend an extra day in a small town as your car is repaired. When you see the signs for Topeka and realize she lives nearby, you impulsively decide to visit your Aunt Edna, whom you haven't seen for years.

Entrepreneurs need to demonstrate the same agility. They can create a business plan just as they can create a route on a map, but they must be prepared to change it when unexpected or unpredictable circumstances arise.

ALLOWING FOR FLEXIBILITY AND VISION IN YOUR BUSINESS PLAN

Entrepreneurs need business plans for a reason. In part, it's to help them create work budgets, strategies, and goals. In part, it's to present potential investors with a document that can induce them to participate, as well as to demonstrate how the company will grow and become profitable after they've made their investment. But business plans offer everyone involved a measure of security as well. The company's goals are spelled out, its finances are listed, and its time frames are defined. Getting this all down in writing—or in a PowerPoint presentation—creates something tangible. Everyone wants to see the business plan, review the numbers, and analyze the strategy. Developing a business plan helps entrepreneurs create a comfort level.

A business plan, however, is a fallible document, especially when it's considered to be written in stone. While you might have to tout the positives of your plan to investors and others, and may well believe it's everything from solid to brilliant, agile entrepreneurs are ready, willing, and able to adapt it when necessary.

An agile plan isn't identified by just what's on the page but also how it's used by entrepreneurs. At the most basic level, flexible business plans are relatively brief and contain estimated date and dollar ranges and execution options rather than fixed dates, dollar amounts, and singular ways of implementing the plan. General guidance rather than highly detailed, step-by-step instructions is the goal. Similarly, flexible plans exist not just on paper but also in ongoing discussions. Entrepreneurs, their teams, and their investors regularly review them and discuss possible changes; they see the plan as a malleable document that can and should be adjusted based on events and trends that impact the business.

As a general rule, the worst, most inflexible plans are:

➤ **Overly Long.** I've seen some that top 100 pages and the sheer volume of words makes it feel like an inviolate legal document rather than an adaptable business plan.

➤ **Written Without Being Articulated.** By this I mean that the business owner rarely if ever discusses the plan in his own words, failing to create excitement about the plan and relying on a facts-and-figures document to carry the load. Being able to talk about the plan in different ways with different audiences is a huge asset. It allows you to communicate what's relevant to a given audience rather than be saddled with a one-size-fits-all document.

➤ **Never Rewritten.** It can take months or years to get a business off the ground after a plan is created. During that time, markets shift, the economy changes, the competitive landscape evolves. Revising a plan doesn't mean you're rejecting your core concept for the business but, rather, that you are recognizing what once was a perfect plan no longer is, for whatever reason. Proud entrepreneurs don't always like to change plans they put a lot of work into and feel strongly about, but it's often necessary.

Plans should not be rewritten without serious consideration, though; this is almost as bad as refusing to make changes! Dialogue, research, and analysis are essential before a plan is revised. As important as your investors are, a reflexive response is ill-advised when an investor points out a possible flaw in your strategy or timetable. Instead, the issue should be discussed with a diverse group of people, and research conducted, if possible, to determine the validity of the proposed change.

In an October 2012 *Inc.* magazine article, journalist Minda Zetlin interviewed William Hsu, the co-founder of startup accelerator MuckerLab and a former AT&T and eBay executive. Offering an agility-friendly perspective on business plans, Hsu advised, "Think vision, not plan. A lot of entrepreneurs . . . have a perfect business plan . . . but that's all they have. . . . They need to agree what the vision is and what the path to success will be. But don't spend time trying to put that into a 40-page document."

I urge you to focus at least as much on the vision as on the document. The former is inherently more flexible, able to be reshaped as the conversation evolves. If you've ever heard an entrepreneur talk about his vision for the company at its inception, a year or two down the road, you're likely to hear two very different descriptions. The hard reality of starting and growing a business affects the vision in many different ways.

HOW GOOD OUTCOMES CAN RESULT WHEN PLANS ARE FLEXIBLE

When taking standardized, multiple-choice tests, the conventional wisdom cautions against changing your initial answer. The reasoning is that your instinct is generally correct and that you'll come to regret replacing your first response with a second choice. Entrepreneurs sometimes use this same reasoning to avoid changing their business strategy and tactics. They feel they need to give their initial concept more time or more money, and that they should have faith in themselves and their ideas and stick with them no matter what.

Though this reasoning is understandable, it's often erroneous. I've found that, in most instances, when entrepreneurs change plans, they do so for good reasons. Often, their changes are in response to testing or initial introductions. This is where the rubber meets the road and where defects in a plan frequently emerge.

The testing or initial phase can be the litmus test for a plan. It doesn't matter whether you're test-marketing a product or service or testing a new market; these are the most common points where you may have to adjust your plans to accommodate feedback from a variety of stakeholders.

Acme Inc. (not the real company name) is a medical company that had created a new technology to help deal with a life-threatening illness; it was one of a number of companies pursuing this technology-based approach. Their plan was solid, but they were waiting for the results of clinical trials before committing significant dollars to product development. When one of the trials was completed, the results were bad, causing a serious drop in the stock price and making it impossible to raise more money. Two competitors couldn't adjust their plans based on their unexpected clinical trial results, and they went out of business.

Even though Acme's stock plummeted when the results of the trial became known, the entrepreneurial CEO reconfigured the company in a number of ways. First, he decided it wasn't worth pursuing the medical product technology and aborted all work on it. Second, the company's research on this life-threatening illness had made them aware of a new drug that seemed to have great promise. The CEO shifted their resources in this new direction, hiring and firing employees so Acme possessed the right talent to take advantage of this shift. Within a few years, they had developed an effective drug, and they were soon bought by a Fortune 100 company for a great deal of money.

THINKING AHEAD WITH A PLAN B . . . AND C AND D

What makes it easier for entrepreneurs like Acme's CEO to change plans is anticipating the need for change. When entrepreneurs analyze what might need to change and what they might do if their plans go awry, they're in a much better position to adjust their strategy. I'm not suggesting you create detailed backup plans for every eventuality, but that you assess the areas where your plan is most vulnerable.

For instance, if your business depends on a technology where your patent is a key to your success, you may want to develop a legal plan in case a competitor challenges or violates your patent. This plan may be nothing more than a "what-if" discussion with an intellectual property attorney, but having even the most informal of plans makes it easier to change course, if necessary. Otherwise, you may be overwhelmed by the implications of the challenge and do nothing until it's too late; or, just as negatively, you may capitulate to the demands of a competitor without investigating your options (i.e., settling a lawsuit quickly so you can maintain the status quo—even though the costly settlement may have been unnecessary).

Some entrepreneurs I've spoken with are reluctant to create back-up plans, in large part because they feel such an action suggests they lack confidence in and commitment to their vision for the business. Perhaps in the past this attitude was understandable, but not today. Young tech entrepreneurs seem to understand Plan B thinking the best, perhaps because they're in a field that changes faster than any other. In an April 26, 2012, *Wall Street Journal* article that reports on the benefits of "pivoting" for tech entrepreneurs, the reporter notes that in the past it took about two years for a company to hire staff, create a product, and determine if the product was viable. Today, "all that typically takes only a few months as founders cycle quickly through different ideas until they find one that sticks." The article explained how Kevin Systrom of Instagram started the company to help people "check in virtually" at various locations via smartphones, essentially announcing to a virtual network where you were and what you were doing. In less than two years, Systrom veered from his original strategy and implemented a new one: a mobile app that allowed people to take photos, change them, and share them. It was an "instant" success and the company was sold to Facebook for $1 billion.

But it's not just young tech companies that benefit because they are prepared to change plans when necessary; this applies to all types of entrepreneurial ventures. You may be familiar with the riches-to-rags story of Boston Market. The company started as a small chain of restaurants in the Northeast in 1985, had a highly successful initial public offering in 1993, and then after a period of expansion it experienced a number of problems and declared bankruptcy in 1998. After emerging from bankruptcy in a much smaller form (from 1,200 restaurants at its peak to 480 in 2011), it was bought and sold twice. It was only when CEO George Michel took the reins and was willing to alter the concept and strategy dramatically that the company started experiencing strong growth. What he essentially did was create a more upscale and healthier experience for customers (no more plastic utensils; servers bringing food to customers' tables; food with less sodium; and other changes) that may have not been in keeping with the company's original core concept but was absolutely essential, given changes in the fast-food business, the economy, and our culture in general.

This couldn't have been an easy decision for Michel or his leadership team; the original Boston Market concept of "good" fast food was one that many in the industry admired and had driven its fast and huge success. But the plan that had worked twenty-five years ago was no longer as effective and the company wisely decided to implement Plan B.

Plan Bs can take many forms. Some of the young tech entrepreneurs referred to earlier seem to manufacture them on the spot, putting their fingers up in the wind and revamping the company depending on which way that wind is now blowing. Other entrepreneurs, such as the leaders of Boston Market, take more time and do more analysis before adjusting their plans.

While agile entrepreneurs should be able to pivot fast or slow depending on circumstances, doing so by going through the stages of discussion, research, and analysis is optimal. While doing something different is often better than doing nothing, you want to do the right thing. To facilitate this outcome, let's look at the most likely ways your plans will be upset and what agile entrepreneurs do in advance of these events.

PREPARING FOR THE UNPREDICTABLE

If entrepreneurs are constantly being surprised by events and situations, and no one can predict many of the trends that come sweeping through the economy, the culture, and various industries, how, then, can you create a Plan B when there's no way of knowing what or when something will impact your business?

While it's true that you can't anticipate many trends and events specifically, you can plan for them generally. You may not be able to predict a new technology introduced in the Far East that will revolutionize your industry, but you can create an alternative plan with steps for researching, incorporating, and adapting that future technology—or any other technology—into your business.

What follows are the most common areas and situations in which your plans may need to be changed, as well as the best ways to plan in advance for these changes.

Key People Leave

For most entrepreneurs, the departure of staff is inevitable. The problem is figuring out who will leave and when. Some entrepreneurs have such faith in the companies and cultures they've created that they can't believe anyone would ever depart voluntarily. Others are convinced that employees won't exit because they possess a powerful financial incentive for staying—they believe, as the owner does, that they'll be rewarded in the form of bonuses or salary increases if the company achieves its goals. As a result of either belief, they don't expect to lose anyone. Entrepreneurs may also fail to create a Plan B because they have included a noncompete clause in an employee's contract or they've threatened legal action against anyone who leaves and "steals" clients or customers. Nevertheless, employees leave entrepreneurial ventures all the time despite noncompetes and other sanctions.

Having a replacement plan in place is crucial. Here are some ways such a plan can be created:

- ➤ Draw up a list of three (or more) employees you can't afford to lose.

- ➤ Identify their most important contributions/skills and who could replace them if they were to leave.

- ➤ Consider whether consultants, freelancers, or other independent operators exist who might be able to replace them temporarily or permanently.

- ➤ Determine if there's someone who works for a competitor whom you might target as a replacement (or if you don't know anyone, contact a headhunter to see if the individual might be able to help).

The Time Frame Changes

You planned your product release for September and manufacturing problems created a delay. Or you banked on your biggest customer placing an order in January as he has done for five years, but this year says he has overstock and won't place the order until June. Or you've banked on being able to complete your new facility in ten months, but because of problems with one of the labor crews, it won't be completed for sixteen months and you've already given up your lease on your current office space.

If there's any truism entrepreneurs should live by, it's that nothing happens as fast as expected. In large public corporations, planning is easier because of their financial resources and clout—they can pay more to get things done faster or call in favors to cut bureaucratic red tape. Entrepreneurs don't always have these luxuries. In their universe, a time frame may be upset by a single individual, such as a supplier's deciding to close his business.

While entrepreneurs can't always prevent delays or other changes to set timetables, they can be sufficiently agile to plan around these anticipated issues by doing the following:

➤ Create realistic time ranges around deadlines and other set dates. Entrepreneurs are often overconfident about their ability to meet deadlines, and when they realize they're unable to do so, they get in trouble. Give yourself more room to meet a deadline by making it flexible. Instead of saying you'll have your company up and running by March 1, create a looser deadline, such as February 15 to March 15. This gives you a cushion should the unexpected occur.

➤ Work up "what-if" scenarios around your deadlines. This can involve asking yourself questions such as: What if I don't deliver the new prototype to our manufacturing facility by a given date? Will this prevent us from getting our product to market before our competitor? If we fall behind in creating the prototype, can we speed up the process by bringing in more people to work on it (and if so, what would be the cost)? What-ifs help entrepreneurs get serious about their time frames and determine which dates are sacred and which are inherently flexible.

An Unexpected Opportunity Emerges

It's not just undesirable circumstances that require entrepreneurs to alter their plans. New markets may surface suddenly, an offer to partner or merge may materialize out of nowhere, or a sudden influx of funds may allow the company to be more ambitious in its strategy. Taking advantage of these developments requires great agility—perhaps even more agility than is required to respond to unwelcome and unanticipated situations. It's relatively easy to gain acceptance and support for revised plans when problems arise. Most businesspeople will recognize that the company needs to make changes in order to recover from them. Responding to unexpected but desirable circumstances may be more ambiguous. There may be debate about how promising an emerging market really is. Your investors and partners may not all agree that a wonderful merger opportunity is really that wonderful.

Changing plans in the face of an opportunity can require entrepreneurs to make a compelling case for a new approach. They may need to be agile not just in what they plan to do but also in how they intend to present their new plan. Jean-Claude, for instance, was a psychiatrist/entrepreneur who had created what he termed a "psychologically valid" anti-smoking program. Through various connections, he had attracted a number of investors and was in the process of creating an anti-smoking kit, website, and advertising program when he heard about two other anti-smoking programs designed by psychologists and built on the same positioning. Worse yet, one of the programs was being run as a subsidiary of a large public company and the other had far more funding.

Jean-Claude could still have moved forward with his original plan, but the more he learned about his competitors, the more uncertain he felt. He decided to meet with a marketing consultant and explain his problem. The consultant studied the situation, did some research, and said that if he were Jean-Claude, he would target a market he believed would be better suited to him, given his expertise. Jean-Claude had done a great deal of work with individuals who had eating disorders, and the consultant told him that a growing niche in this field was pre-teens.

Targeting the parents of these pre-teens with the same type of kit and marketing approach as the anti-smoking effort sounded like a winner. Jean-Claude created a new plan, presented it to his investors, and they not only bought into this change but also recruited other investors to provide him with a much larger advertising budget. The initial test of the company's new product was successful and they are currently in the process of rolling it out to other markets.

If you find yourself facing an opportunity and considering a change of plan, here are a couple of agile ways to respond:

➤ Research the opportunity thoroughly. Sometimes, opportunities sound great when you first hear about them but digging deeper into what they entail may reveal flaws. If necessary, bring an expert into the project to help research the pros and cons of the opportunity. Discuss the research with your advisers and partners. You can never be 100 percent sure how real the opportunity is, but you can avoid making a blunder based on too much sizzle and too little steak.

➤ Test your new opportunity-seizing plan. While it's not always easy or inexpensive to test a revamped strategy or concept, it's often a worthwhile investment of time and money. Though it may be impossible to know if an opportunity has legs until you put something into the market and see how customers respond, targeting a specific geographical area or segment of that market can limit expenses and provide a better sense as to whether the opportunity is real.

You Lose Your Biggest Customer or Client or a Significant Amount of Business

Whether you are losing your best customer or client to the competition or seeing an erosion of your market over time, you most likely didn't expect or plan for that to happen. It's possible to recover, but if you don't have a Plan B as an alternative, that recovery is much less likely.

Here's a cautionary tale of a company (names have been

changed) that didn't plan for an unexpected situation. Company XYZ was run by Nancy, an entrepreneur who formerly had worked for a U.S. government agency in an executive capacity and then left to do consulting work for a number of government groups. When Nancy later created a new company designed to produce a product that she knew the government required, her plan was to be its sole supplier and make a significant profit with relatively little overhead. Nancy's business plan was impressive and she quickly rounded up a solid group of investors. The biggest hurdle in-volved receiving government approval as supplier of the product, and though Nancy and her team had to deal with some red tape to obtain this approval, they finally got it. As expected, when the first order came into Company XYZ, it was sizable. Everything seemed great—until the company's government contact informed Nancy that henceforth, and perhaps forever, the government would buy the product from another supplier that could sell it to them for less money.

Nancy was shocked. She hadn't seen it coming; her competitor turned out to have better connections with the government than she did and was farming out some of the product manufacturing to a group in Asia that could keep the price low. Nancy had no Plan B. Had she been agile, she would have recognized that, at some point, the government might decide to change suppliers and she could have developed her supply chain in the private sector and adapted the product for use by private companies. But she hadn't, in part because she was in love with the simplicity of her plan. Company XYZ was out of business within a month after hearing the bad news.

To avoid hearing similarly bad news, plan for the loss of customers or clients by doing the following:

➤ Create a "diversification" plan to implement in the event

that you lose a key customer or customers. Typically, entrepreneurs can broaden their strategy in some way, whether it entails going after smaller companies, having prospective customers in other geographic regions, or teaming with another company to make their selling proposition relevant to a wider audience. While there's no guarantee this back-up plan will work, it's a better strategy than bemoaning the loss of a major customer or pinning all your hopes (and the company's fate) on targeting a single customer that can bring in similar revenue.

➤ Draw up an emergency cost-savings plan. For many entrepreneurs, a significant business loss is difficult to take because there's not much time to restore lost income. Entrepreneurs often cut it close, financially speaking, especially in relatively new operations. Your goal should be to buy the company time to make it through a difficult transition while you try to replace the income it has lost. Have a plan ready to go that identifies areas where costs can be cut without hurting the company. There are numerous ways of doing this, including reducing the company's staff or cutting entertainment expenses and travel. With the proper planning, it may only take you a few months to replace the business that was lost.

A New, Game-Changing Trend or Technology Emerges

Here's another cautionary tale every agile entrepreneur should heed. Research in Motion (RIM), the makers of the BlackBerry phone, enjoyed market dominance from 2003 to 2007 with its wireless mobile device, but when Apple introduced the iPhone in 2007, its superior technology and ease-of-use changed the competitive landscape in the category.

At the time, however, RIM failed to deviate from its plan. The company no doubt had faith that its extraordinarily loyal users (the term "Crackberry" was coined to describe the addictive nature of the device) would help them withstand whatever technological advantages the new generation of mobile phones possessed. Even as Apple's competitors began incorporating the new technology into their devices, RIM resisted. As a result, the company lost a huge amount of market share, and as of this writing, they're still scrambling to recover just a fraction of the market share they lost.

While it's often difficult to predict significant new trends or technologies before they emerge, entrepreneurs can take these steps to change strategies quickly and effectively when these trends and technologies surface:

➤ Monitor competitors' moves, industry research, customer surveys, and other developments that might impact your business. This monitoring may seem obvious, but most entrepreneurs most likely take only one or two of these actions. All too often, they don't track all these areas regularly. In some instances, they give the monitoring assignment to a junior person or outside consultant who isn't sufficiently diligent. By making a consistent, comprehensive effort to watch for everything from emerging technologies to shifts in customer preferences, you can stay on top of changes that will affect your company. In this way, you get a jump on the competition when it comes to shifting your direction to coincide with major changes and developments.

➤ Rate the impact of the new technology or trend on a 10-point scale. This is a simple device designed to motivate you to create and implement a new plan. With 10 representing the greatest impact, determine if the new development is likely to destroy your business if you don't respond (10), will significantly reduce your revenues if you pursue a business-as-usual approach (5), or will have little or no impact on your company during the next few years (1). Anything from 5 to 10 should compel you to shift your approach in some way.

PUTTING CONCEPTS INTO ACTION

To assess whether you're doing a good job planning for the unexpected and unpredictable events that are bound to befall your business, see how many of the following statements apply to you:

- ❑ We review our plan regularly with our team and have vigorous discussions about its merits and deficits.

- ❑ We changed a significant aspect of our plan at least once during its first year of existence.

- ❑ We've already targeted some potential replacement candidates should any of our top people were to leave.

- ❑ If a customer gave us a new, earlier deadline or demanded we finish a project in record time, we have a new process we could implement that would accelerate our work pace.

- ❑ We have developed resources (individuals and organizations possessing skills/knowledge we lack) that we can draw on if new business opportunities surface.

- ❑ We are confident that we can survive the departure of a major customer or another similar business loss because we can implement tactics that are likely to bring in new business relatively quickly.

- ❑ To ensure that we stay on top of new trends and technologies, we are constantly looking at trade media, research papers, conference announcements, and other sources of information to see if there are any developments that will impact our business.

CHAPTER 5

Exercising Funding and Financial Options

Complexity demands agility, and few entrepreneurial areas have become more complicated than raising money for a business. Before the 2008 recession it paid to be aggressive and single-minded. Many entrepreneurs funded their companies by seeking money from venture capital firms or through bank loans. It was a relatively straightforward process, and while other options existed (i.e., Small Business Association loans), most entrepreneurs fixed their sights on a single funding source and pursued it vigorously.

In addition, entrepreneurs could often estimate with a reasonably good degree of accuracy how much money they'd need to start and run their business during its first year of operation, and even for a few years after that. In an economically stable environment, they could project their costs and revenues for a limited time frame, and unless something unexpected occurred, their projection would often be in the ballpark.

Today, however, economic, technological, and industry volatility makes this rigid attitude a problem for entrepreneurs. Time and again, I've heard stories from small business owners starting new ventures who were certain they had all their funding lined up—until suddenly they didn't. Just as concerning, I've witnessed entrepreneurs who discovered during their first year of operation that they had run through all their available cash in less than six months because of unexpected expenses (i.e., the need to speed up production owing to the sudden appearance of a competitor with the same type of product).

Agility can help entrepreneurs handle these financial ups and downs effectively. Let's look at how this is so, starting with increased awareness of and ability to capitalize on multiple funding sources.

BECOMING AWARE OF FUNDING OPTIONS

In a volatile environment, shifting funding requirements often takes entrepreneurs on roller-coaster rides. Here are just some of the events that have impacted the financing of new or relatively young businesses:

➤ An angel investor reduces the amount of money promised to a new company by 50 percent, owing to his own financial problems.

➤ The venture capital firm that provided funding for an entrepreneur's last two successful startups, and had offered verbal assurance that they want to fund the third one, suddenly declines involvement because a new firm policy requires a higher projected return than they've received from the entrepreneur's other projects.

➤ Within six months of introducing a new product, a supplier raises prices significantly due to problems obtaining a key material from an African country beset by civil strife.

➤ An entrepreneur creates an app that proves hugely popular during the company's first year, but competitors are already starting to create knock-offs, and the entrepreneur needs a major infusion of funds to capitalize on and expand her initial success.

The combination of these and other unexpected events and the multiplicity of funding options makes agility imperative in this area. The first and best step an entrepreneur can take is to become aware of all the possibilities. To help create that awareness, what follows is a list of entrepreneurial funding options, accompanied by some observations about their pros and cons.

Venture Capital

As I've noted earlier, venture capital (VC) funding became much more difficult to obtain after the dot.com bubble burst of 2001–2002, which was complicated further by the 2008 recession. Entrepreneurs sometimes have their hearts set on convincing a big venture capital firm to invest in their enterprise; more often than in the past, they have had their hearts broken. This doesn't mean you should ignore this financing possibility, but you should educate yourself about the new realities. For instance, you can expect any venture capital firm to conduct much more extensive diligence reviews on you and your company than in the past. You can also expect them to negotiate a tougher deal with more stringent requirements (i.e., earlier dates for meeting revenue goals).

While you can obtain lists of top venture capital firms online at http://techcrunch.com/2011/05/25/top-10-vc-firms-investor-rank/, it's difficult to approach VC firms blind these days, no matter how terrific your startup might be; they often prefer to invest once a company has established itself. Still, you may want to give VCs a shot, especially if you're in a hot tech area or have a strong track record. Given the increased selectivity of these firms, targeting is a good approach. Compile a list of venture capital firms that have invested in other companies in your industry over the last five years. Typically, VC firms develop preferences for specific industries and types of products and services. They may be more inclined to talk with you and give you money if you're in their preferred group. Perhaps even more important, tap into your professional service firm network for contacts to venture capital groups. It's likely that your lawyer, accountant, financial planner, stockbroker, or consultant knows a firm executive, and that referral will increase the odds of you getting a meeting.

Angel Investors

Unlike venture capital professionals, angels are more likely to invest early, so it's appropriate to talk to them about startup funds. But they can and do become involved throughout the life of a business. Be aware, too, that angels come in all shapes and sizes. Typically, they're high-net-worth individuals who may be accredited investors, or part of an investor group, or simply be among an entrepreneur's circle of family and friends. On the positive side, angels often offer more favorable terms than other lenders and tend to invest in the person at least as much as in the business—they seek out entrepreneurs who seem to have the magic touch. They also are more likely to focus on the long term than other investors, wanting to help the business become a sustainable enterprise rather than make a quick profit and get out.

If there's a downside to angels, it's that they may become more involved in the day-to-day operations of business than other investors; they may take on a partnership mentality, which can be irritating to some entrepreneurs.

A good site for more information about angel investors is the Angel Capital Association (www.angelcapitalassociation.org).

Crowdfunding

Kickstarter is probably the most well known of crowdfunding sites, but many others have arisen in recent years and they provide an alternative funding source for entrepreneurs seeking to raise modest amounts of cash (typically, less than $100,000). As you probably are aware, these sites serve a "matchmaking" function, hooking up investors with people who have ideas for businesses and other ventures. This tactic is best suited for entrepreneurs with high-concept businesses such as creating a new alternative fuel source based on hydrogen technology. They can convey the nature of the business in a quick, impactful sentence. For instance, it probably won't be an effective tactic if your business is complex or unsexy—if it takes pages of explanation to convey why it's viable or if it involves something mundane, such as the manufacture of widgets.

Loans or Lines of Credit

Most of you know the ins and outs of obtaining loans and lines of credit from banks and other financial institutions. What you may not realize is that there are other ways to use these methods to obtain funding. For instance, some companies obtain lines of credit from vendors—the deal often involves making a vendor your exclusive supplier in exchange for a line of credit. Others strike deals with state agencies where they receive loans using their technology as collateral. For example, states like North Carolina and Pennsylvania have agencies that will loan money to entrepreneurs in areas like biotechnology. The loans are intended to support achievement of specific goals defined in advance by the company.

Equity Financing

This is a broad category, in that it can involve selling a small percentage of the business to friends and family in order to raise a few thousand dollars or an initial public offering (IPO) from a hot entrepreneurial company like Google or Facebook. While equity financing can take different forms, many startups tend to use various equity instruments during different stages of the company's evolution. To attract angel investors and venture capital people to a startup, for instance, it makes sense to offer convertible preferred shares rather than common equity—convertible shares have greater upside potential and provide some downside protection.

When the company grows, it may consider selling common equity to institutional and retail investors. Later on, a sizable entity may want to try secondary equity financings, such as a rights offering or an offering of equity units that includes warrants as a sweetener, allowing investors to buy stock at an exercise price that may not expire for years (theoretically, they can buy the stock low and sell high in the future).

Syndicates

This is just a fancy name for two or more individuals or groups coming together to fund a company. For the typical entrepreneur starting a company with limited resources, a syndicate may simply mean gathering together a few high-net-worth individuals who believe in the entrepreneurial idea and are willing to fund the business in exchange for a piece of the action. This can be an excellent tactic for small business entrepreneurs who are frustrated by the insufficiency of their bank loan or other singular funding source. By creating a syndicate, they spread the risk for investors and increase the odds of obtaining more money than they would if they focused on a single entity.

On a larger, more sophisticated level, syndicates may include a variety of professional financial groups that form a temporary coalition to fund an entrepreneurial venture that no single entity is willing to fund on its own. By pooling resources and sharing risks, groups like investment banks and venture capital firms can place a bet that the company will eventually go public or be sold—a bet that can pay off handsomely if either event occurs.

Specialized or Government Grants and Loans

Depending on your business and background, you may be able to supplement the monies you have by applying for grants and loans from state and local governments, as well as from industry-specific groups, small business associations, the military, and not-for-profit foundations. While you may not be able to obtain large sums of money from many of these groups, it may be easier to get some money from them because you're essentially a "preferred" applicant. Unlike many entrepreneurs, you served in the military or your product may help manage a particular disease, giving you a leg up when applying for grants or loans from these groups.

I also urge you to explore various local and national small business loan and grant programs, since they often have special programs that may be tailor-made for your specific area of the country or type of business. For instance, the Small Business Administration (SBA) runs the Small Business Innovation Research program and provides phased-in grants for significant sums of money—a maximum of $150,000 to explore technological feasibility of a given idea or product and a maximum of an additional $1 million to develop the idea or product if it proves feasible.

Licensing or Partnering with a Corporation, Vendor, or Customer

We live in a collaborative era, and agile entrepreneurs are open to collaborative opportunities. These can involve licensing technology in exchange for cash, creating arrangements with vendors where you receive free supplies or services in exchange for a percentage of the company, or working with a large company on a business that benefits them in some way (i.e., helping them gain a benefit edge through a new service or technology).

FIGHTING FINANCIAL BIASES AND REASSESSING PRIOR FUNDING METHODS

To develop an agile perspective when it comes to all these funding options, you must both fight against any funding prejudices you might have and be open-minded about any funding methods you have considered tried-and-true.

Fighting against funding prejudices means rising above your financial biases, whether it's your belief that venture capital is the only funding source worth going after or that small business loans are for small-minded businesspeople. Force yourself to consider every financing option objectively. It may be that your bias had some validity years ago, but today, multiple-source financing is an essential strategy for many entrepreneurs, and to capitalize on it, you have to let go of your preconceived beliefs.

Being open-minded about funding methods you have considered tried-and-true means being willing to explore previously unexploited funding sources. Entrepreneurs who have successfully started other businesses using a single funding method want to continue to rely on this method. As understandable as this reflex is, it can cause you to be myopic about raising money for your venture. What worked in the past probably won't work in the present because so much has changed in recent years. Look at this situation from a positive perspective: Entrepreneurs have never had so many different ways to fund their enterprises. To capitalize on them, you may need to depart from your standard financing formula, as George discovered.

In recent years, George started four different technology-related companies, all of which had been successful. In each instance, he had received funding from venture capital firms. But each startup came with more onerous requirements than the previous one—the venture capital firms set terms that required companies founded by George to raise capital as quickly as possible and created a situation where he was extensively diluted in his ownership. In one of the companies, the firms demanded the hire of a new CEO who possessed more experience in the industry than George had. At this point, George felt as if he were no longer in charge of the companies he created—that he was not allowed to grow them in a way and a pace that he desired. Just as significantly, he was finding it difficult to make any money with the terms imposed upon him by the venture capital firms.

But when an opportunity came along to start a new company,

George immediately called one of his usual venture capital firm contacts to discuss how much money they might give him and what their terms would be. He then discovered that the terms were even worse than the ones another firm had imposed on him in the previous business. Still, he considered contacting other firms until he read in a report that the amount of venture investment funds available to entrepreneurs had shrunk by one-third from the amount available in 2000. That shocked George into considering alternatives.

After assessing his options and having conversations with various types of investors and lenders, George decided to focus on angel funding. He found a few high-net-worth individuals with whom he developed strong relationships and who promised him that they were in it for the long haul—they wanted to be part of creating sustainable enterprises. Though they didn't provide him as much money as the venture capital firms had, George was able to make up the difference with grants and small business loans. Not only did this give him a greater percentage of ownership and fewer operating restrictions but he was also able to focus on long-range plans for growing the business.

George further demonstrated his agile thinking by launching an initial public offering (IPO). Typically, this wouldn't have been a consideration for most entrepreneurs in George's position (the company was too young and untested), but he recognized that his technology might be considered "hot" and that it might be hot enough to create an effective IPO. He was right, and pulled in millions of dollars through this strategy. Not only that, he made his angel investors happy, since they derived an exit option from his IPO success in which they could leave with the company enjoying a higher valuation than it had when they originally invested.

MANAGING THE DILUTION-VALUATION PARADOX

When it comes to financial agility, entrepreneurs not only have to consider all funding options but they also must learn to manage the dilution-valuation paradox. Typically, rigid entrepreneurs choose either dilution or valuation. Some small business owners are eager to dilute their ownership of the company and that of investors by issuing more stock or attracting more investors; they want to bring in additional dollars to grow the organization, sacrificing short-term value for long-term sustainability. Other entrepreneurs are focused on increasing the current value of the company, or keeping a tight lid on spending while trying to build up the company's assets. Some valuation-oriented entrepreneurs refuse to consider bringing in investors. For them, total ownership is essential; they want to maintain maximum value and have complete autonomy.

Finding the right balance between dilution and valuation is the mark of an agile entrepreneur. In the past, it was easier for entrepreneurs to choose one or the other. Years ago, it wasn't unusual for an entrepreneur to build a company slowly and carefully, refusing to spend one penny more than was necessary and relying on profits to fuel growth. Today, there are too many costs and risks associated with building a business for most entrepreneurs to go it alone. Unless they already have significant funds accumulated and are willing to risk some or all of it, it's usually necessary to acquire other investors to give a business a fighting chance of success.

In the go-go 1980s, high dilution was a more viable option because unlimited growth seemed possible for entrepreneurs. They assumed that, sooner or later, they'd reap a substantial return on their investment through an IPO, acquisition, or merger, or by the company's growing by leaps and bounds. Consequently, they thought nothing of selling off large pieces of the company to various investors.

Today, agility helps entrepreneurs navigate the twin needs of long-term growth and current value. There are times when it makes sense for entrepreneurs to bring in additional investors at crucial growth points of a business (i.e., when an opportunity develops to capitalize on an emerging market), and there are instances when it's crucial to spend conservatively and increase the business's worth (i.e., when the company is the target of an acquisition by a large corporate suitor).

Here are some suggestions that will keep you sufficiently agile to manage the paradox of dilution and valuation:

➤ **Recognize that your approach to dilution and valuation should depend on the stage your business is in.** In its infancy, a business needs money to survive. If you have enough seed money to get you through the initial six months or a year— enough to pay staff, office rent, etc.—then you probably don't have to reduce the business significantly. If, however, you're facing stiff competitive challenges and need to invest in technology or bring in people with key competencies, then you may need to dilute the business beyond your comfort level to remain competitive. This involves taking a situational approach to the issue of dilution and valuation rather than a philosophical or mathematical one (a formula for how much dilution is allowed versus business value).

➤ **Be aware that valuation, like beauty, is in the eye of the beholder.** Founders tend to assign a much higher value to companies than do investors. This is perfectly natural—people who start organizations tend to see them in a more positive, less objective light than those who invest in them. At the same time, founders may have greater insight about the company than do outside investors and their optimistic valuation may better reflect reality. The problem is that when you and your investors possess different ideas of what the company is worth, you may clash over the best timing to bring in additional investors to pursue a growth strategy (and dilute the company's outstanding equity). This requires that you and your investors come to a meeting of the minds on valuation and ownership percentages. It demands a willingness to compromise, an openness to considering other people's opinions, and a conscious effort to be objective about what you hear. In other words, it necessitates agility.

➤ **Develop a money cushion for worst-case and best-case scenarios.** Some entrepreneurs will be frugal to the point of denying themselves or their employees decent salaries in order to keep the valuation as high as possible. They will pinch pennies in every aspect of the business to avoid dilution. Years ago, this wasn't an unusual entrepreneurial model. I've heard many stories of small business owners who operated on a shoestring for a year or more before their businesses started making money. Today, this is not a realistic approach.

Part of the problem is business volatility—your biggest customer could go bankrupt, a new competitor could halve your share of the market, or an environmental hazard could surface and cost your company major dollars. Another part of the problem is opportunities—you could have a small window to ramp up production to meet a new customer's needs. Without a financial cushion, you could run dangerously short of cash—the danger being bankruptcy, on one hand, and the inability to take advantage of an opportunity, on the other. Having a cushion makes it possible for you to be flexible in the face of both negative and positive events.

STRETCHING YOUR CASH RESERVES

Realistically, you aren't always in a position where you can build a financial cushion or do anything but struggle to survive. This is the life of an entrepreneur, and you need to be prepared for the ups and downs and plan how to make it through the down periods.

Cash is king in startups, and it still occupies the status of royalty for entrepreneurs further along in growing their enterprises. Having sufficient liquidity is essential for a number of reasons, including paying suppliers with whom you don't have a track record, attracting investors who are drawn to companies with a solid financial base, having sufficient funds to execute key tasks such as hiring skilled people, paying the rent, or building a website.

Yet as many of you probably know from experience, it can be challenging to maintain sufficient cash on hand for all your business requirements. Earlier, I suggested developing a money cushion, and some of you may have thought, "Dream on." I recognize that it may be touch-and-go from a cash standpoint in the beginning of an enterprise, but I also know that there are opportunities to stretch cash reserves that not every entrepreneur takes full advantage of. Consider the following options.

Use Equity

Some of the skilled people you want to hire are relatively well off financially and they believe in the company you're creating. They may be willing to take a risk and receive equity in the company rather than a salary, at least for a given period of time. Vendors, too, may opt for an equity position instead of cash. While equity-for-cash deals will cost you more in the long run, they can keep the cash flowing in the short term.

Spread the Payments

What depletes cash fast are large payments to vendors. Some of these vendors, however, will be willing to allow you to spread payments in smaller increments over time, enabling you to maintain cash reserves. Too often, entrepreneurs are reluctant to make this request. While not all vendors will agree to these incremental payments, some will, and you won't know who they are unless you ask.

Negotiate Reductions

Sometimes vendors will agree to reductions in a bill if you're a good customer. I've known suppliers who have even forgiven a bill or two when entrepreneurs explain the difficult financial straits they find themselves in. It's in the vendor's best interest to provide a reduction or two, especially if he or she values you as a long-term customer. Vendors want to do everything to ensure that you stay in business, and reducing a bill may be a short-term hurt but a long-term gain for them.

Adjust the Timelines

Speed can kill budgets. You're implementing so many programs and projects within a relatively tight time period and the result is that you're strapped for cash. In certain circumstances, speed is crucial—you're trying to beat a competitor to market with a new product. But many times you lose very little by slowing things down and spreading the costs out over a longer period of time.

Stop Paying Bills

I list this tactic reluctantly, and with a caution. Still, desperate times can call for desperate measures. Stopping paying bills is a risk, and in most situations, I would tell you not to do it. But it may be that you have no other choice and just need to get through a rough patch of a month or two. The danger, of course, is that people can sue you to recover what you owe. Most vendors will give you at least some extra time to pay the bills, especially if you have a relationship with them and if you can make a convincing case that you'll have the money to pay them by a certain date.

Raise Capital

Admittedly, this can be a problematic exercise. Desperate entrepreneurs aren't in the best position to raise capital. At the very least, investors will present you with less favorable terms than when you're not desperate. Still, this may be your last resort to keep the business going, and if you believe that infusion of capital will save the business (rather than just postpone the inevitable), then this may be an option worth taking.

PLANNING AN EXIT STRATEGY

At first glance, this may seem like a separate subject from the financial issues we've been discussing, but it actually is integral to any discussion of investors, funding, and financial goals. Planning an exit strategy, for both you and your investors, is essential, for two financial reasons. First, because your investors make clear what they want their return to be and when they want to get it, they need a good exit strategy so they feel comfortable investing in your company. Second, you need to figure out what you want to get out of your work in building a company and when it makes financial sense to leave.

Unfortunately, a rigid perspective prevents financially grace-ful exits. An entrepreneur like Jim starts a business convinced that he's going to build a sustainable enterprise from the ground up that one day his kids will take over when they're older. Jim was, therefore, surprised when a big corporation made him a substantial offer to acquire his company, a local chain of grocery stores, five years after he had started it. Jim turned them down, convinced that he wanted to stay with the company forever, especially because profitability was at an all-time high and the prospects were bright.

Then a big chain, recognizing that their locations were underserved by supermarkets, opened three stores within a half-mile of Jim's stores. Economies of scale and a willingness to operate at a loss initially enabled this competitor to provide customers with better selection and better prices than Jim could afford. On top of that, Jim's oldest son declared that he didn't want to work in the family business. Work became far less enjoyable than it had been, and he contacted the company that had tried to acquire his business to ask whether they were still interested. They were not. Eventually, he had to close three of his five stores, and the other two were generating only marginal profits.

Jim should have had an exit strategy from the beginning. Instead of dismissing out of hand the great offer from the corporation, he should have evaluated it objectively. At that point, he might have asked his oldest son if he wanted to spend his life working for the family business. He might also have considered what would happen if competition ramped up and his stores ceased to be as profitable as they had been.

Entrepreneurs should plan exits for themselves and their investors, even if no one has any immediate interest in departing. Things change rapidly, and everyone must be prepared to exit with the best deal possible for all parties. This doesn't happen without flexibility and planning. Consider the following investor exit strategies and make sure to discuss them from the beginning and then periodically to assess their relevance to your business situation.

Investigate an Initial Public Offering

While this is not as popular a strategy as it was in the years before the recession, an IPO is worth discussing, especially if the market conditions are right for the type of offering you can make.

Explore Merger and Investment Alternatives

These alternatives include reverse mergers into shells, mergers with public companies, Form 10 filings, and special-purpose acquisition companies. There are special SEC-regulated activities for becoming public, and the Form 10 is an SEC filing document that is used to become public some time after raising capital. The Form 10 allows a company to inform investors of plans to become public after closing a financing. It also provides the required information for investors as dictated by the SEC. The special-purpose acquisition is a means of allowing public stock market investors to participate in private equity transactions. In this situation, a company defines general goals of acquiring technology. Funds are raised for the acquisition, and the technology is then located and acquired after the money has been raised.

Consider Selling the Company

Identifying targets in advance for possible sales down the line helps you do these deals in a timely manner. What large companies out there need the products, services, or technology you're developing? Once you launch your product or obtain proof-of-concept data (the data showing your technology may work as a product), you may have enough of a track record to send out feelers to these large companies or at least establish relationships. This option is one of the best ways for investors to leave with reasonable multiples.

Contemplate Licensing Your Technology

This is a more esoteric but viable way for investors to exit with good returns. In some instances, entrepreneurs can license their technology to other companies and receive milestone royalty payments. For some investors, getting payments spread out over time is a better way to receive their return than in one lump sum. A variation on this theme involves royalty buyout firms that acquire a future revenue stream at a discounted rate (they essentially pay an upfront fee and take the risk that future payouts will occur), and they sometimes are drawn to deals where entrepreneurs license technology to larger companies.

These possible exits, which can involve just investors or investors and entrepreneurs, are all worth considering, even if they are never implemented. By being aware of different ways to get your money out of a company, you increase the odds that you'll be able to take advantage of one of them. Awareness of all the options is a hallmark of agile entrepreneurs.

Discussions of exits may strike you as negative thinking or, conversely, pipe dreams, especially when you're just starting out. Typically, entrepreneurs have difficulty imagining they'll leave a company that they've sweated bullets to build, or cannot conceive of growing to the point that there will be anyone interested in acquiring them. In reality, circumstances change significantly from the startup phase to as little as a year or two down the road. Being prepared for these changing circumstances by considering different exists is a wise approach.

Similarly, many entrepreneurs never consider the possibility that their investors may try and push them out. This happens more often than most people think, and it sometimes happens for good reasons. Some entrepreneurs are brilliant at starting companies but not so good at managing them; they want to control everything even when the company grows too large to make that feasible. Investors become aware that the micromanaging policies of the founder are creating turnover or diminishing the capacity of people to be innovative and productive. If the entrepreneur has diluted the company to the point that investors control a majority percentage, they may ask him or her to leave under these types of circumstances.

Agile entrepreneurs must know themselves well enough to recognize whether the company is best served by them stepping aside—whether that means selling their stake or maintaining their ownership and hiring someone else who is better equipped to run the growing company. After all, such a decision may not just be in the investors' best financial interest but their own as well. Do they want a CEO who will never be able to grow the company beyond its current level or do they want someone who has the skills to take it to the next level and beyond? An agile entrepreneur is sufficiently open-minded to ask him- or herself that question and answer it honestly.

PUTTING CONCEPTS INTO ACTION

How rigid or agile are you when it comes to these financial issues? To help you do a quick assessment of your flexibility in this area, what follows are two lists of traits. The first character-izes an entrepreneur who views funding and related financial issues in a narrow, single-minded manner. The second list offers characteristics that suggest a much more open-minded, option-oriented perspective. See how many checkmarks you make on each list and be aware of your rigidity and agility as you deal with the funding and financial issues that confront entrepreneurs regularly:

Rigid Mindset

- ❑ I have always used one type of funding for projects and refuse to deviate from this tried-and-true formula.

- ❑ I refuse to consider cobbling together smaller funding sources, preferring to focus on a single source.

- ❑ I am obsessed with growing the company at all costs and willing to dilute its value dramatically to achieve growth.

- ❑ I am focused on building value to the point of becoming a tightwad; I nitpick expense reports, pay people poorly, and fail to spend money on essential aspects of the business.

- ❑ I operate with little cash on hand all the time; I would be put out of business if there was a dip in sales or if the business incurred any significant, unexpected expense.

- ❑ I never talk about or consider exit strategies with investors; I never plan for an exit from the business.

Agile Mindset

- ❏ I explore multiple funding options besides the one that has worked in the past.

- ❏ I put together a "coalition" of different funders who may provide varying amounts at varying times in various ways.

- ❏ I have an open mind regarding dilution and valuation; I balance the need for growth with the need for increasing the company's worth.

- ❏ I make an effort to build cash reserves; I actively attempt to use different methods to keep the company as liquid as possible.

- ❏ I am selectively frugal, maintaining a close watch on the money going out but willing to spend on mission-critical projects.

- ❏ I have developed and discussed an exit strategy, both for the business and for investors.

CHAPTER 6

Working with Various Deadlines and Milestones

Many entrepreneurs are either overly aggressive or alarmingly lackadaisical when it comes to deadlines. Either they push themselves and their people as hard as possible to meet unrealistic dates, or they ignore deadlines, alienating everyone from investors to customers. In both instances, they commit the sin of rigidity, possessing a singular approach and rarely, if ever, varying from it.

Demonstrating agility around deadlines and other key business dates requires an ability to think about time frames in a realistic but open-minded manner. Some dates, such as those set by governmental regulatory agencies, must be adhered to. Others, such as a schedule to get a product to market, may require some leeway to accommodate unexpected problems. Agile entrepreneurs have the ability to differentiate between these two types of schedules, as well as to distinguish between external and internal deadlines—those imposed by individuals and organizations outside the company and those that the entrepreneurs impose upon themselves. They are able to take a step back and realize that their internally imposed requirements are creating a reckless rush to the finish line.

Perhaps most important of all, agile entrepreneurs are able to speed up or slow down as situations dictate. Before we examine how to develop this critical ability, let's identify some of the common deadlines and milestones that entrepreneurs face.

IDENTIFYING DEADLINES ENTREPRENEURS FACE, AND DETERMINING THEIR FLEXIBILITY

Entrepreneurs must work with a variety of important dates, especially in their first year or two in business. Here are some key dates most entrepreneurs need to consider:

➤ Business plan deadlines and milestones (for everything from product introductions to profit goals)

➤ Production, manufacturing, and launch dates for products

➤ Investor presentations and meetings

➤ Loan repayments

➤ Regulatory filings (SEC, FDA, USDA, NIH, DOD, etc.)

➤ Sales and earnings reporting

➤ Industry-related due dates (i.e., clinical trial enrollments for pharmaceutical industry)

➤ IRS, state, and employment forms filing dates, including taxes and fees

➤ 83b elections (must be filed within 30 days of equity
   receipt related to vesting)

➤ Salary payments

➤ Vendor payments

Entrepreneurs, more than many larger businesses, live and
die by their time frames. People starting a new venture, especially, are not given much leeway in terms of these dates when they
lack a track record. They also may be cutting it close financially,
and so if they don't repay a loan or make a profit by a given date,
their business could be in trouble. Entrepreneurs frequently see
their deadlines as tests. If they can meet them, it indicates that
their business is on the right track. They also are aware that
investors, customers, and others are measuring their progress by
how well they meet their deadlines.

Given the resonance of deadlines they face, entrepreneurs
often become inflexible when it comes to key delivery dates. Agile
entrepreneurs learn how to differentiate between deadlines that
are absolute and ones that only appear that way. Differentiating
can be challenging, though, in part because of those internal
deadlines entrepreneurs impose on themselves.

Tanya was a highly successful health-care entrepreneur who
had founded a number of small but profitable enterprises. She
insisted that the companies she created had to make a profit within a year or she would close them down. In this way, Tanya felt
she avoided throwing good money after bad. A few years ago,
though, she opened a consulting firm that facilitated electronic
prescription systems for pharmacies. During the first year, she
was able to generate few clients and income, and when the one-
year mark rolled around, she decided that the market wasn't
responding and that she should shut down her firm. One of
Tanya's investors prevailed on her to keep the doors open for

another six months; he had strong connections in the health-care field and had heard rumors about a merger between two companies that would create a huge jump in electronic prescriptions. Sure enough, the merger took place, the field expanded, and Tanya's consulting firm received a large influx of new business. Fortunately, Tanya's investor convinced her to be more flexible with her time frame. Left to her own devices, she would have gone out of business unnecessarily.

To make wise decisions in these circumstances, agile investors need to test their deadlines with "what-ifs":

> ➤ What if I miss the deadline? What's the worst thing that can happen?

> ➤ What if I find a way to expand my time frame? How much would it cost me in dollars and effort?

> ➤ What if the deadline is more in my head than a reality? What if I'm responding to my own particular biases and beliefs rather than what is really taking place?

Similarly, some deadlines have more "give" in them than is apparent. This is especially true for regulatory deadlines, investor-related dates, and loan repayments. When institutions and money are involved, it seems like there isn't any wiggle room. I've heard entrepreneurs say things like, "The IRS is going to come down hard on us if we don't meet our payment schedules" or "I really believe that the venture capital firm will replace me if I can't show a profit in line with our business plan projections for next month." These statements may be true. But sometimes these "drop dead dates" have more flexibility than you might think. Regulatory agencies may be willing to extend deadlines for filings and payments if you agree to pay a penalty—a penalty that might be easier for the business to tolerate than adhering to an impossible deadline. Venture capital firms and other investors may talk a tough game when it comes to time frames, but they too are often willing to extend deadlines if entrepreneurs can make convincing arguments. It's often worth the effort to make these arguments and see if some wiggle room exists.

It's also worth noting that there is more than one way to meet a deadline. You can "partially" meet a deadline or milestone and buy yourself more time. For instance, you may be able to ship half of a customer's order on the delivery date and send the other half a week later. Not every customer will accept this arrangement, but some will be fine with it, especially if you sweeten the new deal by providing this customer with a discount for the next order. Some lenders, too, will accept a partial payment (though they may exact a penalty).

Deadlines are often looser than they might seem. To take advantage of the give in them, entrepreneurs must ask themselves and others some questions about how "hard" a deadline really is and be creative in finding alternatives to originally scheduled dates.

LEARNING TO WORK WITH VARIOUS DEADLINE MENTALITIES

Another time-sensitive issue agile entrepreneurs learn to address involves other people and their approaches to deadlines and milestones. Getting work done by critical dates is usually a collaborative process, and if you're insensitive to or angry with people who don't share your deadline mindset, you'll diminish the collaboration.

A majority of entrepreneurs charge toward deadlines like bulls toward red capes, and they become impatient and frustrated when others slow their charge. Invariably, however, they have employees or colleagues who are slower and more methodical in their work styles. They often verbalize their frustration and alienate their people or they push them too hard. In either case, their intransigence about deadlines causes employees to work less effectively, making mistakes in a rush to get a project done or becoming resentful and doing a less than stellar job.

Some entrepreneurs, of course, view due dates with indifference or disdain, preferring to work at their own pace. Their attitude can frustrate the people they work with, especially important people like investors and partners. Like artists, these business owners believe they should have the freedom to do the job their own way, regardless of how long it takes. They have a high opinion of themselves, perhaps deservedly so, and assume that their investors will recognize that they must set their own work pace if they are to achieve ambitious goals. Of course, that's not always the case, and I've known investors who have pulled out of projects precisely because the entrepreneurs they were backing refused to take deadlines seriously.

I'm not suggesting that a deadline-averse entrepreneur should treat these dates with reverence because the investors or partners do, or for that matter, that he or she should suddenly slow down and let his people work at whatever pace they choose. What I am suggesting is that entrepreneurs become more agile in their situational behaviors. If they know they're going to be working with an investor who is a stickler for meeting various dates, then they need to have a conversation at the very start of the relationship during which they discuss their opposing attitudes about delivery dates and reach a compromise. Or, if they can't reach a compromise, then they need to talk about how they're going to handle situations when the investor expects to receive results specified in the business plan and the entrepreneurs ignore that requirement. They need to figure out a way to manage that situation, such as resetting the deadline immediately after it's missed, perhaps via a conference call.

By discussing these issues far in advance of the fateful day when something is due, entrepreneurs are less likely to offend key business allies and avoid becoming frustrated with the pace of people who work for them. Both parties will have fair warning about each other's work styles and can extend that initial conversation to an ongoing dialogue that avoids upsetting surprises.

AVOIDING DATE INFLATION

Entrepreneurs tend to love their presentations, whether given to investors, customers, or any other group. They sell hard out of necessity, attempting to build enthusiasm that will translate into financing, sales, publicity, and profitable new relationships. While entrepreneurs have to use hyperbole at times to make strong impressions, they sometimes end up believing their own rhetoric. Entrepreneurs become so revved up about their projections and their company's future that they virtually brainwash themselves. That's when they become rigid, especially with respect to delivery dates. As a result, they unnecessarily lock themselves into dates that are often unrealistic or cannot be met.

A fine line exists between working overtime to meet an important deadline and working overtime with little or no expectation that this date can be met. Entrepreneurs need to recognize that raising stakeholder expectations and then failing to meet them can be disastrous. They will be doubly disappointed if they were depending on receiving goods or services or a financial return on their investment on a promised date and that promise was broken. It's far better in these instances to set realistic dates from the start, or to have a tough conversation with stakeholders afterward explaining why these dates have turned out not to be realistic.

More specifically, to avoid date inflation, the agile entrepreneur should do the following:

➤ Think and plan in advance of a big presentation or meeting so that dates are set before the excitement of the moment sets them for you.

➤ Provide date ranges, rather than specific due dates, when possible. In some situations, a hard date must be met. In other instances, however, you can propose a date range for consideration—a range of a week, a month, or even longer. This provides a flexibility that will increase the odds of being able to deliver as promised.

➤ Re-evaluate deadlines and milestones regularly with your team (or with outside consultants) to keep date inflation in check. Once you have informed your people of dates that have been set, periodic meetings with them will give them an opportunity to tell you if they are on schedule. If not, they may be in the best position to help you recalibrate your various key dates through discussion and debate.

NEGOTIATING IMPOSED DEADLINES

Many small business owners are skilled at negotiation, yet sometimes they shy away from negotiating deadlines imposed by others. This reluctance may be attributable to pride—not wanting to admit that they can't make a deadline. It can also be attributable to stubbornness, insisting to themselves they will move heaven and earth to deliver on time, even when it's highly unlikely that even a celestial nudge can help them meet a deadline.

As I've suggested, it's possible to negotiate even if you're dealing with a governmental regulatory agency. It's not possible to bargain with any group or individual, though, if you don't try. Terri learned this lesson the hard way after her small medical products company licensed new ultrasound technology from a local university. As part of the deal, the university insisted on certain require-ments, including that funding be secured for product development within one year after the license was granted. The university also set milestones for the development of the technology by Terri's company, as well as dates for sales results.

At first, Terri was confident she could meet all the required deadlines. Everything was proceeding smoothly until one of her angel investors had a heart attack and died. He had promised a large amount of funding delivered in three equal increments, but he died after only one increment was paid. Terri had no written agreement with him and, as a result, she found herself short of the money needed for development with the one-year mark fast approaching. Rather than tell her contact at the university about her problem, she kept trying to raise the money from other sources. Her fear was that if the university found out that her angel investor was no longer contributing the full amount she had listed in her licensing document, they might pull the plug prematurely.

When the one-year deadline arrived and Terri lacked the funding, she assumed the university would deny her company use of the technology. She arrived at her meeting with the university representative prepared to dissolve her company, since there was no way she could succeed in this highly competitive field without the licensed technology. When she told the representative of her failure to meet her contract date due to her angel's death, he was disappointed but sympathetic. He surprised Terri by grilling her on the progress made to date on product development (rather than just telling her that he was ending the relationship), and then, satisfied with the progress, he asked if Terri would be will-ing to pay an additional 5 percent beyond the agreed-upon amount if they extended the deadline by six months. He also volunteered a good source he thought might be able to help with the funding.

Terri was flabbergasted. She had been under tremendous stress for months, assuming that "all was lost" if she couldn't meet the one-year funding time frame. In fact, she probably could have negotiated the agreement months earlier and reduced her stress considerably. She simply hadn't understood that an extension on this particular deadline was negotiable.

While not every deadline is negotiable, some are, and to capitalize on these situations, do the following:

➤ At the very beginning of a deal, question whether the dates can be moved if circumstances change. Pose likely scenarios that may impact the deadline: the possibility of some of the funding not coming through or an anticipated slowdown because of a complex manufacturing process. In essence, you're setting the stage for negotiating the date somewhere down the line. It may not be necessary, but broaching the subject at the beginning increases the likelihood that the individual imposing the deadline will be amenable to date bargaining.

➤ Assess and use your leverage. It may be that you possess little or none, especially if you're dealing with a regulatory agency or have a small loan from a big bank. In other instances, the company or individual responsible for creating the deadline may have a significant amount at stake in terms of finances or even status, or that you've made money for the deadline-maker in the past and the person owes you. It may be that the other party is the one with whom you got into a particular business in the first place.

Whatever the story may be, you possess leverage because of your history or relationship with investors and other groups. Remind the deadline-maker of what's at stake and how stretching the deadline might improve the odds of his getting a return on that investment. Refer to a discussion you had with him at the beginning of the project and how he was the one, say, who insisted you could have the business up and running in nine months. Use this leverage rather than complain about how the deadline is unfair or plead for an extension. Most people don't respond well to whining or begging, but leverage is something that might buy you more time.

➤ Trade for time. Agile entrepreneurs recognize that they may have to give something up to obtain an extension. Ask yourself two questions: (1) How much additional time do you require? And (2) Is what you have to offer in exchange equal to the amount of time you need?

If you just need an extra day or two, you probably don't have to offer much—a slightly increased financing rate or return percentage for investors. But if you require weeks or months, then you need to sweeten the offer. In some instances, you might have to offer a lot, such as a larger percentage ownership of the business. You might have to promise to pay a relatively large penalty for being late. You might have to think more creatively if you lack the ability to trade financial incentives for time. Perhaps you can offer your services at a discounted rate for some other project where the deadline-maker needs help. The group that imposed the deadline may want to take advantage of your technology or your people for some other purpose. As long as you have something worth trading for time, it's also worth putting it on the table if that can mean the difference between success and failure.

KEEPING YOUR EGO IN CHECK

At the start of the chapter, I emphasized that entrepreneurs must distinguish externally imposed deadlines from internally imposed ones. This is easier said than done. When small business owners are starting up what they believe to be a "hot" business in a highly competitive area, they often create unnecessarily tight time frames. They honestly believe that their deadlines and milestones are dictated by the market, but they are actually set by their highly aggressive, competitive nature.

One of the best examples of this unrealistic deadline setting has occurred in the alternative energy field. More specifically, we've seen many entrepreneurs create electric car companies, convinced that if they get to market fast, they will be the big winners in the field. Yet many of the early electric car entries have had serious design and other problems, and a lot of them have gone under or delivered less than impressive results. Coda, one of the first of these companies, filed for bankruptcy. Aptera folded. Bright Automotive went under. Fisker Motors, perhaps the most promising of the bunch initially, has experienced numerous problems, from design flaws to lawsuits. Though there's no guarantee these companies would have succeeded if they had spent more time developing improved products, they probably would have increased their odds for success.

Agility is difficult when you're unaware you're imposing deadlines on yourself and others that are overly difficult to meet. Again, there are times when tight deadlines are necessary, but it's crucial to assess whether the dates you set are out of necessity or out of aggressiveness, insecurity, or a desire to please others. In terms of the last reason, I know a small, entrepreneurial video game company that managed to form a partnership with a much larger corporation. The head of the small company, Jim, was excited about the partnership. He thought it represented a rare opportunity to combine his company's creative skills with the larger company's resources. The partnership agreement called for an initial project where Jim's group would develop a game prototype and the larger company would test it. If the test went well, they would market it.

During Jim's first meeting with executives from the larger company, he insisted on extremely tight deadlines. He was concerned that the executives looked at him and his group as amateurs and he wanted to show them that they could move as quickly as the larger company could. When Jim communicated his time frames for game development, the executives were impressed and asked if he was sure he could meet the milestones leading up to the deadline; Jim assured them he could.

But despite his group's best efforts, they fell behind schedule, victimized by the usual game development gremlins—various technical glitches that required time and testing to resolve. Jim placed tremendous pressure on his people and some of them felt that the glitches resulted in part due to that pressure. When Jim missed his milestones, the executives at the company shifted their attention to other projects. Though they still wanted to work with Jim's group, they had given the partnership a lower priority because they didn't feel they could depend on him to deliver what he promised.

The advice here is simple to offer and difficult to follow: Don't let your ego get in the way of setting realistic deadlines. Entrepreneurs need their ego to succeed—they're often Davids operating in a world filled with Goliaths—and they rely on their self-promoting abilities. But ego can get in the way of agility, especially when it prompts the setting of overly ambitious deadlines.

Take a step back when you decide on an ambitious deadline and determine if that date is fair—for you, your people, and your partners/investors/customers. Ask whether it will take a miracle to hit the dates you've decided upon or if they just require a strong effort and a bit of luck.

PUTTING CONCEPTS INTO ACTION

If you're like most entrepreneurs, you probably haven't given much thought to how you deal with the various time frames under which you're operating. Assessing your attitude and actions relative to milestones and deadlines can go a long way toward increasing your agility. When you develop awareness of your behaviors regarding these dates, then you're less likely to get locked into a behavioral pattern—a trait of rigid entrepreneurs.

Evaluate your time frame attitudes and behaviors by answering the following questions:

❑ What types of deadlines cause you the most anxiety or give your business the most problems? Regulatory filing requirements? Loan repayments? Meeting investor requirements? Your own internally generated objectives?

❑ How do you respond to this anxiety or these problems? Do you drive your people and yourself to the breaking point in order to meet deadlines? Or do you take a more laissez-faire approach and miss deadlines routinely, figuring that you can always get extensions?

❑ Do you ask yourself "what-if" questions in order to determine the ramifications of meeting or missing a set deadline? Do you think and talk about what might happen if you were to ask for an extra week from the person or group setting the deadline? Do you examine whether the deadline is "real" or one that you've insisted upon because of your aggressiveness or anxiety?

❑ Do you engage investors, business partners, employees, and others in discussions about how you deal with deadlines and other key dates and how they deal with them? Do you have this conversation well in advance of the key date? Do you find a way to compromise with your clashing styles or at least agree on some techniques to manage them if they become an issue?

❑ Are you guilty of setting highly ambitious deadlines in a spur-of-the-moment speech or conversation? Does your enthusiasm for your business or project cause you to exaggerate your capabilities and create due dates that you later regret when you think about them objectively?

❑ Do you usually try and negotiate time frames with various outside groups—investors, banks, government agencies, customers, suppliers—or do you assume they are hard deadlines? Do you find that your pride or stubbornness prevents you from broaching this topic?

❑ Are you honest with yourself when it comes to time frames? Can you step back and think objectively about your motivations for setting a certain date?

If you find yourself answering these questions in ways that concern you—that suggest you have a rigid attitude toward various due dates—then that's a great first step toward becoming more agile. Often, all it takes to develop deadline agility is recognizing that you're being stubborn and narrow-minded. If you're disturbed by this realization, you'll be motivated to change—to ask the what-if questions, negotiate deadlines, and do the other things that increase your flexibility.

CHAPTER 7

Repurposing Products, Services, and People

In a fast-changing, technology-driven world, relatively few things remain successful for long. A profitable product is rapidly eclipsed by one that works more effectively, is more eco-friendly, or costs less. A great service that customers embraced as cutting edge suddenly seems old-fashioned, replaced by a competitor that offers more options and has a better image. A sales executive who had a highly successful career finds that his skills are no longer in demand and his area of sales expertise is no longer needed by his company or others.

Rigid entrepreneurs view these situations as obstacles to their success and try to push past them, improving the product positioning or packaging, updating their services, and working harder. Agile entrepreneurs see these situations as opportunities to tap into new markets, new ideas, and new skills. They find alternative paths and skirt the barriers or avoid them completely. To put it another way, they take advantage of repurposing. I'm using this term *repurposing* in a broad sense to suggest that existing products, services, and people can be reinvigorated by changing them in some way.

Repurposing has been a concept that's been around for a while, especially in the product area. In the early fifties, a company turned a rocket coating into a household lubricant, which we know today as WD-40. But in the Western world, and the United States in particular, repurposing wasn't a widespread strategy because we had become a disposable culture; when something stopped working, our reflex was to get rid of it.

In today's more environmentally conscious times, we have realized that recycling has its benefits. From an entrepreneurial standpoint, we've learned that it often makes financial sense not to toss away something that is losing effectiveness but instead to find another purpose for it. This requires agility, since we often become angry or frustrated when our prized products, services, or people cease to function as they once did. Instead of fighting against reality or just giving up, agile entrepreneurs assess whether a way exists to revive them in new forms.

INTRODUCING THREE CATEGORIES OF WHAT MAY BE REPURPOSED, PLUS ONE

Not everything or every person can be repurposed. Some products or services simply can't be reformulated or reconceptualized, or they demand more time and money than they're worth. Some people are so stuck in their ways that they'll resist any attempt at retraining or working at something outside of their comfort zone. While agile entrepreneurs can't always make lemonade out of lemons, they are willing to explore repurposing possibilities rather than dismissing them out of hand. They will ask themselves whether it's possible to reengineer a product, service, or person (literally or figuratively, as the case may be) and if it's worth the investment.

The three aforementioned categories of what may be repurposed will be discussed in more depth below, after which I'll discuss the "plus one."

Products

Many products have multiple possible uses, and through repackaging, remarketing, and redistribution they can be changed to meet the needs of a fresh market. Perhaps most famously, a scientist at 3M was attempting to create a stronger adhesive and accidently created a weaker one instead. The newly created glue languished for years until another 3M employee used it to secure a bookmark in a hymn book. Suddenly, another use for the glue became apparent, and Post-it Notes were born.

Often, chemists take the ingredients of one product and repurpose them to create another. The air freshener Febreze is made from a beta-cyclodextrin that binds molecules and has been used for everything from dietary fiber to drug delivery. Nitroglycerin, a well-known explosive, has been adapted for use to relieve angina-related symptoms. Warfarin, originally a pesticide used against rats and mice, was later found to be effective as an anti-clotting drug. And plant-derived curare is used by tribes in South America on arrows and spears to paralyze animals during hunts, and somewhat similarly, curare-based ingredients are now used as muscle relaxants during surgery.

Agile entrepreneurs know their products backwards and forwards and are either aware if their products have other uses or they bring in scientists or research and development experts to explore whether other possible applications exist. Sometimes, it requires a certain amount of experimentation or tinkering before a new purpose is found. For years, diodes were key components of various electronic products like radios and power converters; they were valuable because of their ability to have low resistance in one direction and high resistance in the reverse direction. Scientists tinkered with these diodes and discovered that they could use them to emit light. Light-emitting diodes (LEDs) are now replacing incandescent bulbs because of their high energy efficiency.

Services

In many ways, services are less costly and less difficult to repurpose than products. Sometimes, all it takes is a small shift in how a service is positioned or to whom it's positioned for it to become a major revenue producer. In recent years, companies offering private meteorological services have boomed as they took their basic service—providing weather forecasts—and began specializing those forecasts for different markets. Pellucid, for instance, targeted the golf market, providing managers of golf courses (among others) with information about which days in a week are likely to be playable. AccuWeather's Weather Data Services provides companies in the transportation industry with warnings about bad weather that can impact shipments. Financial services companies have also repurposed what they offer customers. Companies like TD Ameritrade offer the typical group of brokerage services but they repurposed them by also offering them online. Other brokerage firms repurposed their offerings by offering discount brokerage services.

Taking traditional services and repositioning them by offering them at discounted rates or providing electronic access are two easy methods of repurposing. If you think about it, apps are nothing more than electronically repurposed services. It's also possible to take a service and give it a new name and purpose without essentially changing the nature of the service. For example, some real estate companies have brokers who provide homeowners with advice about how to increase the value of their homes by rearranging furniture, removing clutter, and so on. By terming this service "staging," these companies, as well as entrepreneurial offshoots, have created viable new revenue streams and businesses. Upscaling is another way agile entrepreneurs are able to repurpose their services. Spas, for instance, have simply recycled the services that used to be provided by beauty parlors, steam baths, and some health clubs, providing luxurious touches that allow them to charge higher prices than those other groups did in the past.

People

This is the most open-ended of the categories, in that people can be repurposed in a variety of ways. Entrepreneurs can seek new skills and knowledge by going back to school or attending workshops and seminars, among other means. Their learning enables them to start a new business or add new products and skills to their existing businesses. Truly agile entrepreneurs can switch fields or professions, translating their entrepreneurial ability from plastics to software, from accounting to analytics. In addition, business owners can help their people learn new skills and acquire fresh knowledge so that they become more valuable to the business. Entrepreneurs are often motivated to help their employees repurpose when their particular skill set is no longer needed or they request assistance in acquiring more marketable competencies.

George, for instance, was both an MBA and a lawyer who decided to repurpose his career. Though he had two prestigious degrees, he found that he didn't want to work for a big corporation or practice law. What fascinated him was biotechnology, a hot field at the time. Rather than go back to school for a degree that would help him get a job in his field, George researched different technologies and found one he thought was highly marketable. He then contacted scientists he knew who educated him about the technology, and he hired a few drug development experts in his particular area who were skilled at creating biotech and pharmaceutical products. Within a year he had acquired funding and is now running a biotechnology company that has a profitable drug on the market.

I would be remiss if I didn't point out that I repurposed myself. With a Ph.D. in chemistry, I started my career working for government laboratories and then worked in labs in the private sector for fifteen years. When an opportunity arose to start a company, I grabbed it; though I had scant business management experience, I recruited a board and advisers who could help me learn the ropes as I ran the business. I've been running companies and helping to raise funds for other businesses ever since, using my entrepreneurial agility to become proficient in areas in which I had no formal education or training.

Plus One

As promised, I want to address the concept of "plus one," or repurposing an entire company and turning it into something new.

Terri, a nurse and physical therapist, started and ran a company that provided personalized rehabilitation services for people who had been injured on the job. Many of her clients were manufacturing companies. As more and more of these companies closed in the United States and opened (or contracted with) overseas facilities, Terri's business dropped off. At one point, Terri had forty employees, but she was down to fifteen when she decided to repurpose.

Terri realized that she had developed significant expertise in workplace injuries, especially in terms of identifying who was responsible for a given accident and projecting medical and other related costs during the rehab process and beyond. So she decided to partner with an attorney who specialized in worker's compensation cases and to provide expert testimony in these cases. Within a year, her company's profits were back to what they had been at the height of her old business, and within two years they were 20 percent higher. Providing expert testimony was a much more profitable business model, even though the number of workplace accidents had decreased as companies moved their manufacturing facilities overseas; she was able to charge a much higher fee for the expertise of herself and her people within the legal system context.

While it's difficult for large, established organizations to repurpose themselves, it's an opportunity that agile entrepreneurs can capitalize on. When a company is small and young, it is inherently more flexible than a big, bureaucratic structure. It can be reconfigured with new or altered products, services, and personnel. It can take advantage of its talent and business relationships and direct them toward more marketable opportunities. There's no shame in this. Some entrepreneurs I've counseled are wary of taking this path, feeling that jettisoning their main product or service is an admission of failure. But neophyte companies often experience growing pains and need to fail once or twice to find a profitable path. They aren't being wishy-washy or fickle by changing what the company is about—they are being agile.

Sometimes, a company just has to swallow its pride and repurpose. One of the best examples involved the catalog company, Spiegel. For many years, it was known for offering inexpensive products to a lower-income market, but this positioning became less effective in the seventies as large discount stores provided stiff competition. With bankruptcy looming and no way to turn the company around as it was presently constituted, CEO Hank Johnson decided to do a total corporate makeover. Though the company retained its catalog, it changed what it sold, how it sold, and to whom it sold. Using the slogan "from crass to class" and poking fun at itself rather than acting ashamed, the company targeted an upscale market of professional women with high-quality products—especially name-brand and designer clothes—and created a glossy, highly stylized catalog that looked nothing like the old one. It was a huge success, and even though the company lost many of its old customers, it built a successful new foundation due to its repurposing.

PAYING ATTENTION TO UNEXPECTED POSSIBILITIES

Repurposing isn't always a simple, logical process. While it's great if entrepreneurs recognize that a product's life span is limited and that it can be rebranded or reconstituted to take advantage of a growing market, the process isn't always this neat.

Sometimes you just need to heed the signs and investigate. I've discussed in a previous chapter how Ashleigh Palmer was working at an anesthesia subsidiary of a large industrial gas company when an inventor approached him with an idea for using a gas pollutant to treat babies suffering from lung disease. Someone with a rigid mindset would have dismissed the idea out of hand, as Ashleigh's parent company did. But Ashleigh possessed an agile perspective and so he did his research and discovered that, as unlikely as it might have seemed, this gas pollutant might be a highly effective treatment for this condition.

Being agile means being open to alternatives, even those that seem unlikely. It's difficult to imagine that a product, service, or person we've nurtured might exist in the world in a different, more viable form; or that we can succeed in a slightly or significantly different field. Yet entrepreneurs have nothing if not imagination, and when considering alternative purposes, they should apply it.

For instance, Daniel had spent the first twenty years of his adult life as an entrepreneur, starting a series of software and technology companies that did very well during his first decade but became less successful in recent years. Part of the problem, Daniel knew, was that he had fallen behind the technology curve and it was difficult for him to catch up. Another part of the problem was that he'd lost at least some of his youthful energy and resourcefulness. It took Daniel a long time to recognize these facts and that maybe his purpose should shift. Fortunately, a friend of his was associated with the urban planner for a large city who was looking to start a technology incubator in association with a local university. They were searching for an executive director of the incubator and had already hired a search firm and were interviewing candidates. The more Daniel learned about the job, the more he realized he was ideally suited for it. Though he had to get his head around a future of not running a company and being an executive director, he finally saw the light and has flourished in the position ever since.

Sometimes, necessity is not only the mother of invention but also of repurposing. Jana was a Polish immigrant who came to this country as a single mother of three; she spoke little English and needed to make a living. A friend of hers had been cleaning houses in a wealthy suburb but was going to get married, have children, and stop working, so she began referring her customers to Jana. Jana soon had a thriving small business and recruited other Polish immigrants to help her expand it. At one point, she had ten women working for her and was doing well, but then she began losing customers to a national home-cleaning chain that charged less than she did. Though most of Jana's customers were private households, she also had one commercial customer—a small motel on the outskirts of the suburb where her business was located.

Jana and the motel owner were talking one day when he explained that a number of motels and hotels in the area were finding it difficult to find and keep good cleaning help; that the workers they hired would leave suddenly without notice. The motel owner also told her he suspected that some of these companies wanted to outsource their cleaning services owing to their dissatisfaction with the quality of cleaning they were getting. Jana realized there was an opportunity to repurpose her residential services as commercial by focusing on her area's hotel and motel industry. Within a year she had revived her business, and within two years was earning almost twice as much as she had when she just had residential customers.

Ashleigh, Daniel, and Jana are very different types of entrepreneurs and they repurposed in different ways. But what they all shared was a willingness to depart from an established path. They were able to view a product, a service, and a career in a fresh light. None of them could have predicted that they would change paths the ways in which they did. But they were open to the unpredictable rather than looking at it with suspicion or doubt.

USING CHANGE AS A CATALYST FOR REPURPOSING

You can't repurpose in a vacuum. More precisely, you can't try to capitalize on a new version of a product, service, or person if nothing has changed. Change is the catalyst for repurposing. When a person's skills no longer are marketable, it's time to learn new skills. When a product or service is eclipsed by a new and improved version, it's time to analyze whether it can make a comeback by re-introducing it in a new form or to a new market.

Entrepreneurs often ask me when the best time is to repurpose. While this answer can vary based on many factors, a good guide is to watch for changes in each of our three categories. If you can spot these changes early and anticipate how they might affect you and your company negatively, then you can capitalize on the repurposing opportunity. Let's examine the changes you should watch for in each of three categories:

Product Changes

➤ Competitive products that have come out recently have significantly higher quality or more features customers want; there is no way to adapt your product so that it can regain its competitiveness in any of these areas.

➤ A product category is on a downward slide because of negative media coverage, new technologies, or a fading fad.

➤ Low-cost competitors enter your market (from overseas or domestically) and it's impossible to sell at the new price without going bankrupt.

Service Changes

➤ Other companies can provide greater speed of service in response to customer demand; you can't match that speed.

➤ The service you offer has become outdated; a new and improved type of service is replacing the traditional service.

➤ It is becoming increasingly difficult for you to continue to sell your service at a profit (often because of rising overhead—primarily staff—and declining pricing).

People Changes

➤ You find that your knowledge and skills that helped build your business (or businesses) no longer are as useful as they once were; you lack the expertise required to help your company solve the problems it faces.

➤ Your enthusiasm for running your company is waning; you require a fresh start or challenge in order to re-engage.

➤ Some of your previously productive employees have lost their value; you find it easier and less expensive to outsource their jobs or discover that their jobs are no longer necessary to the company.

None of these changes guarantees that repurposing will be a success. You may have nothing to repurpose to; you may lack a viable way of reusing your product; or you are strapped for cash and can't afford to retrain your people. Change is nothing more than a signal that repurposing is a possibility, and it's a signal that agile entrepreneurs heed. At that point, they then need to figure out how to repurpose.

THE THREE Rs OF REPURPOSING: REPOSITIONING, REDIRECTING, AND REJUVENATING

Repurposing can be as simple as a name change or as complex as creating a new business. Suggesting how to repurpose, then, can be a bit tricky because circumstances can vary widely. Nonetheless, I've found that everyone can benefit from three guiding repurposing principles: repositioning, redirecting, and rejuvenating.

Repositioning

Repositioning means shifting how a market perceives a product, service, or even an entire company. This can be accomplished through traditional marketing tools—ads, sales promotions, and public relations—and it can involve an orchestrated campaign using social media. The substance of the product or service remains the same, but its image is repurposed. For instance, low-calorie beers and sodas used to be sold as beverages that facilitated weight loss. Many of these beverages have been repurposed through advertising so that they are now perceived as hip or sexy or cool, and the original purpose of a lower-calorie drink is subordinated or even ignored. On a smaller scale, an entrepreneur can create a more upscale image through a product packaging redesign, or the entrepreneur can publicize all the pro bono work his or her company is doing so customers with the same mindset are attracted to his products.

Repositioning is a relatively inexpensive tactic (unless you're a huge company like Coca-Cola repositioning one of their sodas through multimillion-dollar ad campaigns), but it's one that is not always possible or useful for entrepreneurs. It may be that there isn't a viable way to reposition your product or service; for example, you sell widgets and the limited ways to reposition them have already been taken by competitors. Agility means considering all options, so it's worthwhile to assess this one—if it's not feasible, then you move on to a new one.

Redirecting

Redirecting involves taking an existing product or service and moving it in a more marketable or profitable direction. Agile entrepreneurs determine whether a product or service can be:

➤ Sold under a different name with a different product or service benefit to a different market from the current one; Ashleigh Palmer's example is one illustration of this, creating a new use for an industrial gas by developing it as a pharmaceutical product that saved children's lives.

➤ Transferred from one medium to another to reach a new audience; the Ameritrade example indicates how a company can move a product online and profit.

➤ Changed so that it solves a new problem; Warfarin went from being used to deal with the problem of rat and mouse infestation to solving the problem of blood clots.

Rejuvenating

Rejuvenating requires adding an energizing element to the existing product, service, or person. The new and improved version of a product may possess something that makes it taste better, work faster, or perform more effectively. Car companies often rejuvenate a model whose sales are sagging by improving gas mileage or giving the car a more attractive design. Entrepreneurs do the same thing. Jelmar, a small entrepreneurial company that makes household cleaning products such as CLR and Tarn-X, gave their products a boost by making their entire line of products "green" by removing phosphates and taking other steps that earned them positive reviews from environmental groups.

Perhaps the classic service rejuvenation is Pandora, a company that reinvigorated music streaming by allowing people to develop personalized, evolving "channels" through innovative technology. Other companies followed Pandora's lead, but they repurposed a service in a variety of ways, including providing two subscription options (free subscription accompanied by advertising; or a fee-based, advertising-free service).

People, too, can be rejuvenated through training and education or by shifting to a job or career that renews their commitment and creativity. I previously related the story of a commercial real estate agent who went back to school in his fifties. He learned the skills required to be a project manager for software development, as well as other projects. He is now a huge success and assists Fortune 500 companies in employee training. As for me, I certainly felt rejuvenated when I moved from working in government labs to running my own business.

LICENSING TACTICS

If you possess sufficient agility when it comes to repurposing, then you're able to expand the search beyond your own company's borders. Specifically, you can capitalize on the discoveries made by universities and other research institutions. They possess brilliant professors who conduct academic research on alternative fuels, cutting-edge technologies, alternative medicines, and in many other areas. They often take out patents on what they discover and invent, but they may lack the wherewithal to commercialize and monetize their discoveries. As a result, they are open to partnering with outside companies, from the world's largest to its smallest entrepreneurs. In many instances, their discoveries are purely academic in nature, but savvy entrepreneurs can repurpose them into profitable products via licensing.

You can find the right university or research institution technology to license in two ways:

1. **Search the patent database.** Obviously, you can't search it randomly hoping to find the proverbial needle in a haystack. You have to have a sense of what you're looking for and its commercial possibilities. Let's say you're a health-care products entrepreneur and you've seen a number of studies about the possible harmful effects of dental x-rays. You suspect these studies will soon be publicized and there will be a market for dental x-ray machines that produce lower doses of radiation, so you scour the database looking for an institution that filed a patent for this type of machine or technology related to developing such a machine.

2. **Search institution listings for available technologies, inventions, and research.** Universities and governmental research centers often have technology transfer offices you can contact to see what they're willing to license. Many of these institutions have websites that list what's available and provide the names of contact people to initiate discussions. Again, you can't conduct this search blind. You need to have at least a general idea of what research area you're looking at in order to create a specific product. If you're interested in developing a new solar panel, then you can search websites and contact technology-transfer offices that have done research in this field. It's also possible that a large corporation possesses technology that they're willing to license to entrepreneurs, though this can be an expensive proposition.

Licensing is a great tool for agile entrepreneurs, but be aware it always comes with a cost. Universities and other institutions may not drive as hard a bargain as for-profit companies, but they still want to obtain fair value. Be aware, too, that just because you want the license doesn't mean they will give it to you. The institution granting the license will take a long, hard look at your experience and expertise before making an agreement, and that agreement may include "clawback" provisions that will allow them to take back the license if you fail to develop the technology or other discovery/invention within a reasonable time frame.

As a repurposing tactic, licensing may not be for every entrepreneur, but it's often an underused one due to rigid thinking. I've talked to entrepreneurs who have told me they never considered licensing because they were certain that no university would consider them worthy licensing candidates or that they couldn't afford the cost. While these and other reasons may be valid, agile entrepreneurs are willing to test their validity. For instance, while the cost of licensing does scare away many entrepreneurs, what they don't realize is that in certain situations they can obtain licenses for no initial cost. For instance, they may be able to obtain an option to license a targeted technology or include a milestone date within the contract that allows the institution to reclaim its rights if you can't raise the capital necessary for product development by that date. In the latter instance, you essentially possess a repurposing idea backed by a technology or other work created by a prestigious institution. This gives you leverage to round up capital you might otherwise lack.

PUTTING CONCEPTS INTO ACTION

Are you willing and able to repurpose some aspect of your business or yourself? It's entirely possible that you've never given this question serious consideration. As I noted earlier, some entrepreneurs feel as if reconceiving a business, product, service, or skill set is an admission of defeat; they are loathe to admit that their strategy didn't work or they are missing key skills. Some entrepreneurs, too, operate with blinders. They are so focused on the goals they've set they don't see that these goals are no longer achievable based on what they're selling or how they're selling it. Consequently, they don't see the value of repurposing.

To answer the question that began this section, consider some other questions that may help you recognize if or when you might repurpose:

- ❑ Have you (or your advisers) suggested that your products, services, people, or organization are "stuck in the mud"? Have they implied that they once were dynamic, profitable, and cutting edge and now they aren't anymore?

- ❑ Do any of your products have uses that you've never communicated to customers? Do any of these uses seem more marketable than the use you currently emphasize?

- ❑ Do you offer services that might benefit from making them faster, or more efficient, or by adding an element that you know customers have been requesting?

- ❑ Are there people in your company whose areas of expertise have become less valuable over time? If you could magically transform them into skilled employees with a different area of expertise, what would it be?

- ❑ Do you feel you would become a more effective leader and manager if you gained new knowledge and skills? What would they be? If you possessed this additional expertise, might you use it to create a new company or move to a new field?

❑ What are the three most significant changes that have affected your business in the last year or two? What have been the consequences in terms of profits? Are these changes likely to become permanent or have an even greater impact in the future?

❑ Is there a way to respond effectively to these changes through repositioning, redirecting, or rejuvenating? Do you feel that pride or stubbornness has prevented you from using one of these tactics to make your company more successful?

❑ Is there a way you might shift your company's strategy or focus so that it would be more profitable? Can you think of different ways you might create that shift? What could happen if you were to target a new market or change the company's image?

❑ Are you aware of research going on in universities or other research institutions that might benefit your company? How might your company benefit if you had access to cutting-edge technologies? Would you be willing to pay a reasonable amount of money to license a given technology? Do you feel you could raise capital to develop products based on a technology that was better than what your competitors are using?

CHAPTER 8

Overcoming Entrepreneurial Inflexibility

The degree of agility that entrepreneurs exhibit is rarely constant. It fluctuates based on factors such as recent business successes or failures, personal financial losses or gains, the economy, and obstacles and opportunities your business is facing.

You may demonstrate a high degree of agility when you start a business and continue to try new and different approaches for a period of time, but then you introduce a new product and it fails miserably. Or you have a personal financial setback and it makes you paranoid about a professional failure. Or a competitor enjoys tremendous success with a new product or service, prompting you to respond with a knockoff product rather than pursuing your own vision. Undesirable situations can prompt you to avoid risks, reject innovative options, and fail to consider a diversity of ideas and opinions.

However, you can also be driven to forsake agility for rigidity when there are more encouraging situations. Perhaps your company has had its best year ever and you don't want to change anything for fear of sabotaging your successful run. Or you believe you've discovered the key to success—a strategy or tactic you think is foolproof—and as a result you're reluctant or unwilling to vary your approach.

Being aware that you can fall back into rigid attitudes and behaviors helps you rectify the situation before it becomes too late. Raising your entrepreneurial consciousness helps you make decisions and take action with an eye toward how agile you're being. Recognize that you're vulnerable to rigidity recidivism, and this recognition will keep you alert for signs that you're losing some of your agility.

CONQUERING FACTORS THAT CAN LEAD TO INFLEXIBILITY

Entrepreneurs move from agile to rigid mindsets for all types of reasons, but I've found that certain factors commonly create this backward movement. Typically, they encounter situations or events that cause them to believe that the status quo is preferable to trying something new or that doing nothing is better than doing something. These are often illusory beliefs, but they're also powerful and need to be addressed so they don't have a negative impact.

To maintain entrepreneurial agility, therefore, you have to be able to conquer seven factors that can lead to inflexibility:

1. Vanquishing a disheartening business failure

2. Getting beyond the "foolproof formula"

3. Surmounting complacency after sustained success

4. Surviving personal financial problems

5. Shaking competitive lethargy

6. Defeating crippling indecisiveness

7. Refusing to get stuck in the past

VANQUISHING A DISHEARTENING BUSINESS FAILURE

Failure is scary, and it's natural to have some anxiety about assuming new risk or changing strategy and tactics after being blindsided by a major misstep. It can throw entrepreneurs into a dangerously rigid operational mode, particularly if they have been highly confident, successful business owners.

For much of his career, Carlos was as agile as a world-class gymnast. After receiving an MBA from a top business school, he worked for a large food and beverage company, but hated the bureaucracy and regimentation. Once he had saved enough money, Carlos opened his own business importing gourmet candies and cookies from Europe. His business was successful in large part because he saw opportunities others missed and was adept at testing new products and concepts. Although his business model was as an importer and wholesaler, he saw possibilities in opening retail establishments and switched directions, creating a number of small but profitable stores. A few years later, he made yet another transition, importing a wider range of products from companies in Japan, Australia, and Mexico and selling them to specialty retailers. But then, convinced that he could make a greater profit through direct online sales, he closed his stores and shifted all of his business to an online site.

It was a huge disappointment. Carlos had underestimated how the right retail setting was crucial to selling relatively unknown foreign products at a price that was higher than the norm. He was shocked by the failure and kept beating himself up for his short-sightedness. He told colleagues that he no longer trusted his instincts. When Carlos restarted his business, returning to his importing strategy, he found it was not as successful for him as it had been in the past. Nonetheless, he stuck with it, content to muddle along rather than risk another failure. When opportunities presented themselves, he would reject them, coming up with all sorts of reasons that they were wrong for him. What he really meant was that they required him to stretch himself in a new direction, and for the first time in his business life, this idea terrified him.

Like Carlos, many entrepreneurs aren't prepared to deal with the failure that eventually happens to just about every businessperson. To maintain your agility if or when you fail, keep the following in mind:

➤ **Failure represents an opportunity to learn and grow.** Whether it's fate or your own errors that created the situation, consider that you're acquiring valuable new knowledge and skills. Experiencing failure provides the motivation to figure out why things didn't go according to plan. The productive response is to see it as a chance to avoid making the same mistake twice, and to develop skills and resources that will serve you well down the road. In essence, failure can be a catalyst to entrepreneurial agility.

➤ **Equating risk with failure is a mistake.** Risk will seem scarier once you've failed, and you'll want to avoid experiencing another misstep. But while taking risk exposes you to the possibility of failing again, it also opens up opportunities for success. The key is to recognize that risk-taking can be only one of the causes of failure, which can also include everything from a competitor's innovation to simple bad luck. Acknowledge that you're more anxious about taking another risk, but move past your fear by analyzing the risk you're contemplating in more depth and breadth. Survey people you trust about the risk, consider worst-case scenarios, and explore different ways to manage them (i.e., spreading the financial investment over more partners).

➤ **The vast majority of entrepreneurs survive their failures.** The failure might not seem survivable at the time, and it may result in the closing of a company, but it doesn't stop most entrepreneurs for long. Whatever the financial toll a failure takes, it isn't nearly as devastating as the emotional one. I've known many entrepreneurs who have suffered serious setbacks. But it wasn't a financial obstacle that prevented them from being successful again—it was the rigidity that set in because they couldn't handle the ego-deflating defeat. If you have a good product or service to sell, you'll eventually find financial backing. To capitalize on it, though, you have to develop a survivor mentality. Survivors are inherently agile, doing whatever is necessary to keep going.

GETTING BEYOND THE "FOOLPROOF FORMULA"

There are 1,001 terrific entrepreneurial formulas, but they are terrific only in certain situations and at certain times. If you stick with a formula long enough, it will cease to be as effective as it once was. If you stick with it too long, it will prevent you from considering other options or trying other approaches. Ironically, when entrepreneurs first discover these formulas, they often are highly flexible, willing to experiment with new and different concepts. Inflexibility sets in once they're convinced they possess the secret sauce. They guard it jealously and overvalue it. They believe that if their formula worked once, it will work again, and again, and again.

The best entrepreneurs take multiple shots at a goal, and this is impossible to do if you're clinging to a magic formula. Larry, for instance, is a 74-year-old entrepreneur who has become extraordinarily wealthy due to his willingness to create a staggering variety of startups. He admits that one out of three of his businesses fail, but says that a 66 percent success rate enables him to overcome the financial losses his failures cause. Years ago, Larry had learned the value of switching strategies as situations warranted. Early on in his career, he started a catalog company that sold a variety of products, including gardening equipment, shoes and boots, and wristwatches. When postal rates and paper costs skyrocketed, he shut down his company and moved to a completely different field—selling home and industrial cleaning products. Larry stuck with the new company for about five years, until competition from companies in the United States and abroad prompted him to sell the company to a larger competitor. He then moved into the dot.com business and did well with two different enterprises until the bubble burst. After taking a year to survey various possible businesses, Larry decided to focus on niche software, and has started three different companies in this field.

Not all entrepreneurs can or should be like Larry; not everyone is capable of such radical swings in business models and fields. But it's important to recognize that entrepreneurs are often rewarded when they're able to transition from one business method to another, one company to the next. By not getting locked into a specific way of operating or even a specific field, the agile entrepreneur can avoid settling into a fixed position that may only be viable for only a relatively short period of time.

SURMOUNTING COMPLACENCY AFTER SUSTAINED SUCCESS

For many entrepreneurs, doing well can be both a blessing and a curse. The blessing aspect is obvious, but the curse part stems from the way it locks entrepreneurs into formulas involving structure, process, and strategy. While they may have been risking-taking, innovative leaders in the company's start-up phase, they become conservative and status quo—oriented as the company becomes a sustainable enterprise.

The typical path followed by many successful entrepreneurs running startups includes these steps:

1. They launch a company armed only with a great idea, their ingenuity, and just enough funding to sustain themselves for mere months. They fly by the seat of their pants and improvise continuously to keep the enterprise afloat.

2. After a break-in period, things begin going well and they fine-tune their operation, adjusting the business's focus based on trial and error, getting rid of methods that experience shows aren't viable and implementing new ones.

3. The company experiences growth spurts and the entrepreneur adds people and processes in order to manage the growing enterprise and help the company shift from a growth stage to one of relative maturity and sustainability.

4. Formal structures are established, policies are enacted, mission statements and long-term plans are created, and the pace of change slows considerably, as does the entrepreneur's appetite for risk and innovation.

These steps are common and at times inexorable; creating tools to manage a company becomes more important than implementing ideas in a fast and furious survival mode. As necessary as it is to create policies and procedures as organizations succeed, entrepreneurs don't need to become slaves to them. Finding a balance between structure and spontaneity is the challenge, and one of the best ways to meet it is by doing the following:

➤ **Don't believe your own publicity—literally and figuratively.** When you create a successful, ongoing enterprise, you'll receive plenty of compliments. If your success is sufficiently large and public, the media and investors may brand you an authority or a genius. Even if you enjoy a smaller, sustained success, you'll begin to have greater faith in your expertise. This is fine until it leads to rigid thinking. Consciously or not, you'll become increasingly proud of your accomplishments and may cross over from pride to hubris. When entrepreneurs think they know more than everyone else, they don't invite a diversity of opinions and they become inflexible, neglecting to consider paths and concepts different from their own. Former market leaders like IBM, BlackBerry, and Avon are among the major companies that have been so convinced their leadership position meant they knew more and were better than others that they failed to anticipate and adapt to market changes.

➤ **Recognize the role luck plays in success.** Just as luck can lead to success, it can also turn on you and lead to failure. Agile entrepreneurs are prepared for the time when their luck turns. They do worst-case scenario planning regularly, and though it's impossible to predict all the ways a business can go south, they have done sufficient research and planning that they have flexible strategies in place that can be put into practice if their luck turns.

SURVIVING PERSONAL FINANCIAL PROBLEMS

Many business executives claim they're able to separate their personal from their professional lives, compartmentalizing problems at home so they don't impact the quality of their work. Entrepreneurs often feel the same way, and in some instances they may be able to stop the emotional traumas in their personal lives (divorce, problems with kids, etc.) from affecting their businesses. But entrepreneurs are especially vulnerable to personal financial problems, since the line between personal money issues and their business's finances is so thin. If they have a major personal investment loss, for instance, it can affect their thinking about how they invest in areas of their business.

Jack was a psychologist who became a bold entrepreneur. After a few years as a sole practitioner, he grew disenchanted with his practice, finding that many of his patients needed more practical advice and help with planning than psychologists provided. Taking a course in life coaching, he obtained his certificate and began coaching clients rather than seeing patients. Jack turned out to be an excellent coach; he soon had more clients than he could handle, and he hired other coaches. For the first time in his life, he was running a business with employees. Eventually he hired an office manager, and when the business was doing better than ever, he began creating a long-term strategy to expand it, including creating an online coaching app, as well as a plan to franchise his coaching model.

Then Jack's wife announced she wanted a divorce and was seeking custody of the children. Though he ended up with joint custody, the divorce was costly and his custody and maintenance payments were high. Around the same time, Jack experienced a financial setback because of an investment that failed to pan out. The combination of these two events left him in precarious financial straits.

Jack was shaken by his personal financial downturn, though his business was doing well and eventually he would be in fine shape once he adjusted to his new circumstances. But his concerns about money caused him to cancel the launch of the online coaching app and scrap the franchising strategy. They also caused him to make other moves at odds with his agile mindset, failing to replace one of his coaches when she left the business because he worried about adding the salary to his overhead, and refusing to consider a promising social media strategy to increase awareness of his business.

Jack's story is not unusual. Financial issues at home can have a profound influence on how entrepreneurs manage their businesses. It's as if they're waiting for the other shoe to drop—for their personal financial difficulties to infect their professional fortunes. As a result, they become extremely conservative even when nothing in their business suggests it's wise.

While some situations exist where entrepreneurs need every penny they can save due to serious financial problems, in many instances they become unnecessarily rigid in response. If you find yourself in this situation, keep the following points in mind:

➤ Being an agile entrepreneur is often the best remedy for money difficulties at home. Your ability to run a successful business will eventually help you pay off whatever debts you've incurred and put you back on a sound financial footing. The danger of rigidity is that you allow your personal setbacks to impact your professional success.

➤ Irrational financial conservatism in business is often a sign of inflexibility. Assess the cause of your frugality. It's one thing if the business is going through tough times and strict financial measures are necessary. It's another if the business is healthy and entrepreneurial paranoia sets in.

➤ Entrepreneurs sometimes equate poor personal financial decisions with poor business financial decisions. If they make a bad personal investment, for instance, they begin to question how they're spending money on the business. Therapists call this "stinkin' thinkin'." As traumatic as it may be to go through a personal financial upheaval, it doesn't mean you've lost your ability to lead and manage your company. I've known many entrepreneurs who have made a mess of their personal lives and have remained highly successful, savvy entrepreneurs by maintaining an open-minded and flexible approach to running their businesses.

SHAKING COMPETITIVE LETHARGY

Some entrepreneurs settle into a state of benign competitiveness. Rather than anticipate the moves of their competitors and strike proactively in order to thwart them, they lose their competitive edge. It's not that they're unaware of the competition but because the pecking order has remained the same for a while, they begin to fall into a routine, running the same ads, offering the same promotions, and making the same pitches. This doesn't just happen to entrepreneurs who have grown enormously successful; it happens regardless of success. Typically, the longer the business has been operating, the more vulnerable it is to competitive lethargy. Today's market calls for entrepreneurs to be hyper-vigilant for competitive moves and be ready to act quickly and innovatively.

As an example, two entrepreneurial pharmaceutical companies had similar products that were first and second in their category for years. The number one company had settled into its comfortable position and stopped doing the aggressive advertising and creative promotions that had helped build its success. The number two company remained fiercely competitive. The company got wind of a university study that cited the effectiveness of an ingredient in its product very similar to the one in the market leader's product that helped combat a digestive disorder. The company changed its packaging to focus attention on it, summarized the study for prescribing doctors, used social media, and applied aggressive sales tactics to spread the word about their product and the study. The number one company in the market wasn't aware of the study or even the gains in sales of the competitor for months and then they responded to it sluggishly. The number two company soon became number one.

Agile entrepreneurs don't succumb to competitive lethargy. They constantly monitor research that impacts their business and closely watch what their competitors are doing. Perhaps most important, they plan for different competitive scenarios and develop a quick-strike plan to respond to emerging trends, new technologies, and prestigious studies.

DEFEATING CRIPPLING INDECISIVENESS

Indecisiveness can kill an entrepreneurial business, and to a great extent that's because it causes small business owners to become passive instead of active. Passivity is just another form of rigidity—when you can't act, you're as lifeless as the proverbial stiff in the morgue. This problem is particularly widespread today because entrepreneurs are facing more choices than ever. Many of these individuals grew their businesses by being decisive, able to choose between two options quickly and without second-guessing. Today, these same entrepreneurs don't have two options, they have ten! There are so many possible paths that some entrepreneurs freeze up and choose none of them.

It's not uncommon for startup entrepreneurs to be confronted by multiple investor groups with different term sheets for financing. I've known individuals who have been overwhelmed by the possibilities and struggled to choose one because they feared making a mistake by not choosing one of the others. They were stymied by what is commonly referred to as "the law of unintended consequences"—that if they choose Investment Group A, Investment Group B will end up providing better financing and better terms to a competitor. It's never possible to be certain that a structure will result in being the best. Analysis of the deal structures and groups provides a hint of the better way to go. That said, picking a deal and group does not ensure the optimal arrangement. For example, management changes in the investment group or loss of further investments from that group are always possible. These unexpected issues can alter the company's survival; such issues are always possibilities.

Entrepreneurs fear that Investment Group A's presentation sounds good now but they'll end up in a bitter fight with its lead investor and wish they had chosen Group B. Perhaps they chose the best group but the group forced the sale of the entrepreneur's company too early for the entrepreneur. Countless events may occur later causing the entrepreneur angst! One of the worst deals ever made by a company Robert ran occurred when one of the investors, also a board member, insisted on a particular structure for a business deal to purchase an asset. The deal, completed as requested by the board, greatly contributed to the demise of the company.

Indecisiveness can result from either success or failure. You're on a good run and you're afraid to try anything new or risky for fear of ending that run, or you've made a couple of bad decisions in a row and are now scared of doing anything that might result in a third. You may be able to justify your indecisiveness based on your previous successes or failures, but the danger is that it prevents you from adapting to changing circumstances. You end up fixed on a strategy, policy, or process that no longer fits your company's needs, but you're unable to depart from the status quo owing to your fear of another failure or of tampering with your success.

While there are times when it makes sense to postpone decisions because you want to see how a situation unfolds or need to gather more data before making a choice, these can become justifications for indecision. Being decisive is the agile entrepreneur's advantage over larger, bureaucratic corporations. To use that advantage, learn how to extricate yourself from the bog of indecisiveness by doing the following:

➤ **Solicit diverse ideas and facts.** Consult with advisers, ask other outsiders from professors to various experts for their opinions, expand your reading to gain greater knowledge of the choice in front of you, or do an informal survey to see how things are trending. Gathering this information may not provide the data nugget that helps you decide, but you'll feel more confident about your ability to make a choice having done your due diligence.

➤ **Analyze with risk in mind.** What keeps entrepreneurs from making a choice is their fear that they'll damage or destroy their business. Analyze a decision with worst-case scenarios in mind and think about how you can reduce the risk. Essentially, this is a hedging strategy where you decrease the odds of worst-case scenarios from unfolding and increase your ability to decide.

➤ **Recognize that doing something is usually better than doing nothing.** Many bad choices are fixable before they spiral out of control. If you've done all of the above and still make a decision that has negative consequences, you should be more prepared to deal with them, being well informed about the risks and having considered the consequences. In any case, being decisive helps move your company forward rather than allowing it to become moribund and slide backward.

REFUSING TO GET STUCK IN THE PAST

You may have heard the saying, "Stick with the one that brung you to the dance." Remaining loyal to a concept or strategy that brought initial success makes sense up to a point—the point where circumstances have changed so significantly that it's no longer a viable approach. Entrepreneurs remember their past successes fondly, and are sometimes prone to recreating the past in the present, taking something that worked years ago and attempting to use it again. Sometimes this can work, but in other circumstances it causes entrepreneurs to be repetitive and rigid in their approach to new business environments. Instead of adapting to all the changes that have taken place, they're operating as if nothing has changed, and they are relying on concepts, strategies, and tactics that have fallen out of favor with their target market. Other entrepreneurs convince themselves that some past trend, product, or plan will once again become popular. Rather than changing their ideas to fit changing times, they keep waiting for the return of full-service gas stations, house-to-house personal selling, and the like.

Accepting that the past is gone may seem obvious but it's not always easy to do. Although Barry's background was in financial services, he turned his love of good food into a string of successes with restaurants, finding investors in the financial community who shared his interest and liked his business plan. He believed that, to be successful and distinguish itself from competitors, a restaurant had to find a significant point of difference. His first restaurant was a gourmet vegetarian soup/sandwich/salad café. Investing a lot of money in a top food public relations firm to create a splash, Barry had a hit on his hands. He used this combination of creating media buzz with a differentiating gimmick to open five highly successful restaurants.

But then the formula stopped working. After two failures, Barry was unsure of what he was doing wrong and kept reverting to what had worked in the past. He was about to launch a third restaurant using this formula until an adviser told him that his failure to shift his publicity budget to social media and away from traditional media had become a huge problem. It took a number of difficult conversations with the adviser and Barry's own recognition that he was stuck in the past before he was able to shift his approach and succeed with a third restaurant where other attempts had failed.

The key here is to remember that just as events, trends, and methods continue to evolve, so too must entrepreneurial businesses. To get unstuck from the past, recognize that your thinking does not need to change radically but, rather, incrementally. An evolutionary mindset means thinking ahead and seeing the next generation of a product or a new and improved type of service.

PUTTING CONCEPTS INTO ACTION

Rigidity recidivism is a danger for even the most agile of entrepreneurs. To protect yourself against sliding back into inflexible, status quo–maintaining, risk-avoiding thinking, monitor whether you're shifting from an agile to a rigid mindset. If this is the case, the earlier you become aware of this shift, the easier it is to reset yourself on an agile course.

To facilitate this awareness, keep asking yourself the following questions about each of the factors we've discussed:

A Disheartening Business Failure

❑ How much did a business failure affect you? Do you think

about it constantly, though it took place months or even years ago? Do you find yourself constantly thinking about the failure and beating yourself up over what happened?

❑ Do you find yourself avoiding any situations where the failure might repeat? Have you asked yourself objectively whether your avoidance is based on real marketplace factors or on your own fear of repeating a traumatic mistake?

A Belief You've Discovered a Foolproof Formula

❑ Do you use the same strategies and tactics in every business you launch? Have you been using these strategies and tactics for a significant period of time—five or more years?

❑ Has your field changed in the last five to ten years? Are there new competitors who have been successful with a variety of products, services, and business strategies? Does your formula for success take into account all the changes that have occurred?

Complacency After Sustained Success

❑ Have you been doing well for months or years and worry that you might "jinx" yourself by making changes?

❑ Do you believe that your success can be sustained over a long period of time if you just make sure you do what brought you your original success? Do you know of other businesses that have been able to enjoy sustained success without making changes in product formulations, services offered, package design, distribution channels, e-commerce, and the like?

Personal Financial Problems

- ❏ Have you experienced personal financial losses or cash flow problems as a result of bad investments, a divorce, helping family members, or for other reasons?

- ❏ How have these financial struggles affected the way you run your business? Have they made you worried about taking risks and suffering financial losses in your professional life that mirrors the losses in your private one?

Competitive Lethargy

- ❏ Are you as driven to compete with rival companies as you were in the past? Have you been running the same business for years and if so, has your competitive fire diminished over time?

- ❏ Do you sometimes lack the energy or interest to launch an innovative new concept to thwart a competitor? Do you recognize that you are resigned to your company's position in your industry or category? Do you find yourself co-existing with your competitors rather than trying to beat them?

Crippling Indecisiveness

- ❏ Are there times when you find yourself unable to make a business decision? Have you told yourself that it's better to let things develop as they will rather than make a choice you'll later regret?

- ❏ Are you coming up with rationalizations and excuses for doing nothing, whether it's the uncertain economy or a downturn in your product or service category?

Stuck-in-the-Past Mentality

❑ Do you think a lot about the "good old days" of your entrepreneurship? Do you begin a lot of sentences with, "I remember when . . . "?

❑ Are you waiting for a return to a business climate or situation that existed years ago? Have you tabled a lot of new programs and policies because you're convinced that the business environment will soon be similar to what it was five or more years ago?

PART III

Monitoring and Troubleshooting

You now possess the knowledge and tools necessary to become an agile entrepreneur, but as you move forward, you'll need two more skills: the ability to be flexible as a business leader and manager (and not just as a "doer"), and a perspective that will help you anticipate and respond to change in the coming years.

In terms of the former, think of agility holistically. As important as it is as a business owner to be able to consider all your funding options, it's just as important as a leader to be open to all your people's ideas. In terms of the latter, you should not get locked into your present concerns but broaden your outlook so you're thinking about what might happen down the road and how you can adjust as early as possible to take advantage of this future event.

If you pay close attention to these issues and develop methods for responding to what you observe, you'll possess the all-around agility that will serve you and your business well.

CHAPTER 9

Learning How to Lead and Manage with an Open Mind

One of the biggest challenges facing entrepreneurs is how to become an agile leader and manager. Many small business owners demonstrate great agility when they're scrambling to get their companies launched, thinking out of the box to develop the idea for their business, and communicating a marketable vision to different audiences in different ways to attract and sign up investors. Yet once they reach a certain level of success, some of that agility goes by the wayside.

This is a natural process to an extent. Just as young bodies tend to become less flexible as they age, entrepreneurs lose some of their agility as their business grows and stabilizes. Given time and success, the drive to find innovative approaches to problems or to change strategy on a dime fades, or at least becomes less common.

Not all entrepreneurs get a thrill from implementing a new, creative hiring strategy or from running meetings with an open, diversity-minded approach. Some don't even realize this is required of them. Developing entrepreneurial agility in areas such as team building, strategizing, motivating, and hiring requires a willingness to shift from being rigid to becoming flexible, and this starts with being creative in dealing with tasks that may be viewed as dull or routine.

PRACTICING MANAGERIAL CREATIVITY

As a scientist, I spent many years in the laboratory inventing new products, yet I lacked the same creativity and flexibility when I was called upon to manage areas of the business that grew from these products. Of even greater concern, my willingness to treat some business functions as necessary but mundane tasks caused my employees to mirror my attitude. As a result, no one was able or willing to think imaginatively in an attempt to solve some of the functional problems that beset the company.

Not long ago, I was attending an investor conference when I encountered a hedge fund manager on an elevator. While trading war stories, he told me about a company in New England that had become extremely profitable due to a single invention. Both the company and the product were created by Thomas, the CEO, who was not as good a manager and leader as he was an investor and risk-taking company builder. Consequently, when the patent expired on the product, he had failed to map a strategy that took into account what would happen, and the company's revenue declined precipitously. To make matters worse, he had such faith in the value of his product and his people that he believed the business would rebound once customers recognized the quality of his product compared to the competition, and he refused to consider reducing staff or taking other actions in response to emerging competitors and falling revenues.

It took months of declining revenues to shake Thomas's faith, and it was only when the company narrowly averted bankruptcy that he started considering other options. Working with the hedge fund manager, he came to the conclusion that the company would be better served if he assumed the role of chairman and appointed a new CEO. As chairman, Thomas could restrict his duties to areas where he was inherently flexible while bringing in a chief executive who would apply energy and fresh thinking to essential management tasks. Once the new CEO was hired, he reorganized the business and reduced the staff. These moves saved the company money and helped them launch a marketing campaign and introduce new products that returned the company to profitability.

One of the best ways entrepreneurs can increase their creativity as leaders and managers is by focusing on a specific problem. Wrestling with the difficulty of hiring the right people or of solving a complex shipping issue can force bored or complacent entrepreneurs out of their comfort zone and into a creative one. There's a five-step process that helps scientists creatively problem-solve in the laboratory that is applicable here as well, and I share those steps with you:

1. **Learn as much as possible about the problem.** The more you learn, the more you stretch your mind. Obtain data about the problem, do fact-based research about how other entrepreneurs have handled similar situations, conduct interviews of experts in this particular area. Knowledge is a catalyst for fresh thinking and new perspectives. It may not provide you with an immediate solution, but you'll exercise your creative thinking, which may eventually lead to a solution.

2. **Engage the team, staff, and advisers.** The ideas and opinions of a diverse group can jar you out of your managerial rut. While they may not offer the perfect solution, they may jump-start your creative process through discussion and debate.

3. **Define the ultimate goal.** Verbalize your ideal goal or outcome or put it in writing. This exercise often works best when you create ideal resolutions, no matter how unlikely they might be. This prompts you to work backward and devise different tactics to achieve it. For instance, if the problem is that customers have been complaining about slow delivery of their orders, the ideal goal or outcome might be to deliver all orders one day before they're expected. The solution is to outsource the delivery formerly handled in-house; in pursuing that ideal outcome, you discover a vendor that has a state-of-the-art system that shaves significant time off of deliveries.

4. **Ramp up communication.** Dialoguing with your people helps them feel valued and more willing to offer solutions to the problem. Continuous conversations require effort and time, but they can also give people the opportunity to share information or an idea they otherwise would have kept to themselves. It doesn't matter whether these exchanges take place in person, on the phone, or digitally; as long as they continue, they can spark fresh thinking about a problem.

5. **Step back for a while.** Entrepreneurs tend to be obsessive, and obsessing over difficult problems without clear solutions can create a level of frustration that leads to taking the easiest route or the one always taken. Tabling the problem for a few days or even a few weeks (assuming nothing negative will happen by delaying) can free up your mind to envision a new approach. I often come up with solutions to managerial problems when I'm working out. A cost-effective method to reduce clerical costs that

was so elusive when I was pursuing it arrived almost magically when I went for a jog.

KNOWING WHAT YOU DON'T KNOW AND WHAT YOU DO KNOW

Managing with indifference or ignorance can create leadership rigidity, but so can absolute certainty. Some entrepreneurs dislike specific tasks so they never bother to learn much about that function or area. For instance, Terri was a technology expert who had founded a number of successful companies, but she hated the human resources aspects of the job. Terri didn't like to deal with hiring or promotion decisions, feeling uncertain about her choices in this area, as well as disliking giving people bad news. Because her companies were relatively small, she often didn't have a budget for an HR director, so she would either assign the job to someone else (who usually lacked the requisite experience or expertise) or she made quick, poorly thought-out decisions in order to complete the task as quickly as possible. As a result, Terri tended to hire the first person she interviewed and gave everyone the same bonuses and raises, regardless of performance. Her lack of interest in and knowledge of human resources ensured that she would follow a pattern in her decision making that resulted in a series of bad or mediocre hiring choices.

Other entrepreneurs are absolutely convinced that they know how to lead or manage better than anyone else, so they don't solicit other people's input or question their own decisions. If you've ever worked with someone like Jim, you know this type of individual. Jim ruled his small manufacturing concern with an iron hand, micromanaging everything from machine repair to the phrasing of customer emails. Jim was certain he could handle these managerial tasks better than anyone else because he knew his business inside and out. While he was extremely knowledgeable about his business and his industry, he was not a good situational manager. For instance, he had a policy of sending a stern reprimand by letter to any customer who failed to pay his bill within 30 days. When one of their largest and oldest customers failed to pay a bill within this time frame, Jim sent this letter, despite a request from his sales manager that he not do so; the sales manager explained that the customer had been beset by an unusual confluence of circumstances (tax problems, a lawsuit, etc.) and that he had asked every company to whom he owed money to be patient and promised to pay the bills within 90 days. Jim refused to listen to his sales manager and sent the letter. Within six months, the offended customer pulled his business from Jim's company and gave it to a competitor.

Entrepreneurs like Jim not only display managerial rigidity but they also often prevent their people from being agile. Employees say to themselves, "Jim is going to do it his way no matter what I do or say, so I might as well do exactly what he wants," and consequently they display little initiative or creativity. They do their jobs by rote because their boss seems to care little for their contributions.

Do you run your organization like Terri or Jim? The odds are that your behaviors are not as extreme as either of them, but that you lean in one direction or the other. Self-assessment is necessary to raise awareness of your tendencies. Entrepreneurs who are conscious of their leadership type find it easier to moderate its effects. Look at the following list of traits and see which is closest to your leadership or managerial style:

Terri's Style

➤   Delegates tasks of little interest.

- ➤ Carries out functions (when not delegating) outside of her area of expertise in a desultory or disinterested manner.

- ➤ Makes little or no effort to learn about topics or areas unrelated to her main area of expertise.

- ➤ Fails to inspire employees or help them learn and grow if their functions fall outside her area of interest.

- ➤ Falls into unthinking routines to deal with responsibilities that seem mundane.

Jim's Style

- ➤ Acts authoritatively about everything.

- ➤ Insists that people follow his directives.

- ➤ Fails to include a diverse group of people in managerial discussions.

- ➤ Refuses to consider ideas or tactics that are different from the ones he favors.

- ➤ Becomes angry and even abusive when employees deviate from his instructions.

No leader or manager is perfect, and at times we all display aspects of these two styles. To guard against their rigidity-inducing effects, however, entrepreneurs must make a conscious effort to moderate their styles. If you're an avoidant leader like Terri, try to learn about functions outside of your area of interest and step out of your routines every once in a while. If you're an authoritative leader like Jim, loosen up and give other people a chance to voice their opinions and test their ideas.

BEST PRACTICES OF AGILE LEADERS

In large corporations, there exists a high degree of what I refer to as leadership consciousness. Organizations send employees to executive leadership workshops and seminars and often provide training in various managerial skills. Performance reviews often measure how well people are developing as leaders and managers and reward them accordingly. In most large, public companies, everyone from neophyte managers to senior executives recognizes the value of developing their leadership and managerial abilities—the value to their companies as well as their careers.

In smaller entrepreneurial enterprises, this consciousness is lower or nonexistent. So much time and energy is focused on core issues—product or service development, financials, customers—that leadership development becomes less important. As a result, entrepreneurs and their top people don't work on becoming motivational leaders or communicative, inclusive managers. Instead, they frequently lead and manage reflexively, failing to expand their range of competencies.

Entrepreneurs who develop agile leadership and managerial capabilities tend to adopt four best practices. Let's look at what they are and how they put them to use in their companies.

Carve Out Time Daily to Inspire and Motivate

This can be a challenge for busy entrepreneurs grappling with what may seem like a crisis every hour. It may also require a somewhat uncomfortable interaction for entrepreneurs unaccustomed to motivational exchanges with employees. But the discomfort diminishes with practice and the time required is relatively short.

To inspire and motivate, it's not necessary to get up on a "stump" and deliver a rousing speech (though you certainly can if this suits you). But it will mean interacting in a positive and constructive way with an employee who needs guidance; an employee, perhaps, who is down because his project didn't work out; an employee who is confused about the organization's direction and why you've assigned her a task that she feels is unnecessary; or an employee who may need nothing more than encouragement to continue taking risks and trying new approaches to a problem.

For many of you, these interactions will expand your range of managerial behaviors. Instead of simply working with employees by telling them what to do or asking those informational questions, you're adding another way of relating and communicating as a leader. You're also encouraging your people to be more agile. Your encouragement and support will help them take risks and try new things that they may have felt reluctant to try before.

Rejuvenate Yourself

Entrepreneurs tend not to take as many vacations as professionals who work for other companies. In fact, I've known many entrepreneurs who work seven days a week for long stretches when they're facing deadlines or other pressures. While situations exist when this nonstop schedule is necessary, entrepreneurs sometimes overdo it. They convince themselves they can't let up for a day (or even a second), that they must be in the office or everything will fall apart.

Being driven and working hard has advantages, but they're offset when it results in single-minded, myopic leaders who are so dominant and obsessive that they become predictable, one-note businesspeople. Entrepreneurs who hover close to a burned-out state are as rigid as businesspeople get. As hard as they work, they also labor without much imagination or openness to others. Consumed by the task at hand, they become robotic.

Taking a day, a week, or a month off can restore leadership agility. It doesn't matter whether you spend the time at home or in an exotic locale, whether you go on a great outdoor adventure or a walk in the woods. By reducing stress and getting out of the work environment, you gain perspective. Fresh ideas flow to you when you're not mired in the day-to-day details of running the business. You start thinking broadly and boldly rather than in a frantic, extremely focused way.

Donald, for instance, ran a unique gift store with a range of innovative merchandise (crafts, paintings, gadgets) located on a busy street in a major city. Donald had built a loyal, upscale clientele for over thirty years, but revenues had declined recently, in part because a significant percentage of the business's customers had either died or moved to warmer climates. Donald responded to the falling revenues by working harder than he ever had before; he ran all sorts of promotions, phoned and emailed every customer who had ever bought something in his store, and badgered his salespeople to be more aggressive. For months, he practically lived in the store without any appreciable increase in revenues.

Finally, his wife forced him to take a long-delayed Hawaiian vacation. When they arrived in Hawaii, Donald grumbled that he should be in the store rather than on the beach, but gradually he succumbed to the beautiful weather and the side trips his wife had planned, and he found himself having a great time. During the vacation, Donald commented to his wife that their guides were all very young, and as soon as he said it, he realized he needed to hire younger salespeople who not only could relate better to young customers but would also have a better sense of what sort of gifts might appeal to customers their age. When Donald returned, he hired two young salespeople, and within the first month revenues rose by 15 percent. It was a small and perhaps an obvious tactic, but Donald was too enmeshed in his business to think of it until he rejuvenated and freed his mind to consider fresh possibilities.

Be Creative and Proactive in Rewarding and Recognizing People

It's not enough just to pay employees a decent salary or to pat them on the back for a job well done. Employees yearn to be recognized individually by the boss. They want to feel the CEO is aware of their contributions and values them. This type of recognition makes them work harder and more effectively. More to the point, it offers you a great opportunity to stretch yourself as a leader and as a manager.

Here are a range of ways entrepreneurs I've known have rewarded and recognized their people:

➤ Bob created an incentive stock ownership plan whereby employees are rewarded if the company is successful.

➤ Ella devised financial incentives for employees who finish tasks before deadlines, under budget, or come up with innovative solutions to problems.

➤ Charles developed nonfinancial rewards for job achievements, such one or two additional days off work, an all-expenses-paid weekend vacation, tickets to a sporting event, or a gift of some kind.

➤ Samuel turned a company credit card used to make company purchases into a reward by allowing high-performing employees to select gifts based on accumulated points.

➤ Josephine ran a competition between teams, with the winner receiving a prize (the prize wasn't worth a lot but the fun and challenge of winning a competition were the real rewards).

Step out of the leader/manager role and become a coach. As I've noted, entrepreneurs often base a lot of their employee interactions around instructions—telling them what to do or what they did wrong and how to do it right. Coaching shifts the relationship between a manager and a direct report, and many entrepreneurs fail to stretch themselves in this direction. Coaching is not about giving orders or criticizing. It's about developing a different sort of relationship with employees, one in which you listen, advise, and suggest options. If you have a lot of employees, you don't have the time to coach everyone. Therefore, targeting key employees—usually high potentials who are underperforming for one reason or another—is the best strategy. As a coach, you need to resist your impulse to be decisive, to dominate the discussion, and to issue orders. Coaching is a more collegial relationship than many entrepreneurs are used to, and it can help develop stronger relationships with employees.

DEVELOPING A TEAM MENTALITY

If you're an entrepreneur who hasn't worked in a large organization—or didn't work there for long—you probably haven't been trained in team leadership skills. Perhaps just as important, you may not be a natural team player; you may prefer the rugged individualist mode of working and leading.

Yet being able to select and manage a team increases your agility considerably. Well-functioning teams provide a diversity of ideas. They are often able to accomplish tasks faster and with more creativity than individuals, and they often possess the confidence and drive to take on ambitious tasks that others may shy away from.

To realize these benefits, though, entrepreneurs can't choose teams like they choose their inner circle. They can't just hire like-minded individuals who share their ideas about business and are good at executing tasks. They must look for people with different skills and knowledge, as well as individuals who can engage in productive conflict. This last point proves tricky for some entrepreneurs, since they're eager for their teams to reach consensus quickly and move on. Vigorous debate among team members with different backgrounds and perspectives, however, is how team agility develops. The team members are willing to push each other and consider fresh ideas in order to resolve their problem. They don't settle for what the entrepreneur wants or the easy solution but are willing to look far and wide to find the best solution.

Entrepreneurs must also run these teams with a flexible rather than an iron hand. If you're like the majority of small business owners, you want your teams to work quickly, efficiently, and productively. What you may struggle with is listening to team members voice ideas that seem radical, off-the-wall, or very different from your own. It takes time and patience to develop a tolerance for good team discussions, but I've found that most entrepreneurs can become strong team leaders by doing the following:

➤ Force yourself to allow what seems like unproductive conflict to continue for at least five minutes (or longer). This means staying on the sidelines while the argument persists for whatever time limit is set. In some instances, a terrific idea will emerge from the conflict and that's when you will realize the discord was worth it.

➤ Resolve conflict without playing favorites or embarrassing either party. This means choosing the side that seems right, not the one that is closest to your own views or articulated by someone you're close to. It also means acknowledging the validity and intelligence of the losing side and explaining clearly why you're choosing the other position.

➤ Become familiar with the team's strengths and weaknesses. Team management works best when you know what the team is capable of as well as where it will need assistance. Give a team a task that is beyond its capabilities and its members will become frustrated and unproductive. Give them a job that is too easy and they'll become bored. When teams receive a task that is well suited for their strengths, they usually tackle it with creativity and intensity. They feel comfortable taking risks and considering alternatives when dealing with the task because they know it falls within their capabilities. Similarly, if the team is working on a project and it lacks certain knowledge or resources, your job is to provide it, even if you have to go outside the company to obtain it. Again, if team members feel they possess the tools they need to deal with their task effectively, they're more likely to consider all the alternatives and take reasonable risks for superior outcomes.

DECIDING WHEN IT'S TIME FOR LEADERSHIP CHANGE

Agile leaders know when it's time to step aside. Rather than locking themselves in place and continuing to run a company they're no longer able to lead as effectively as they once did, they understand they need a replacement. Stepping aside can occur in different ways. Sometimes, entrepreneurs kick themselves upstairs and become the company chairman, hiring someone else to be CEO. At other times, they remain as CEO but hire a COO to take over the tasks they no longer are handling as well as they might. And at yet other times, they will leave the company entirely, perhaps serving on the board or even severing all ties with the enterprise he or she created.

There is no right new role to step into or way to do it; there is only a right time to depart. Entrepreneurs may know it's time because they make a serious blunder—they invest a lot of money in a product introduction that fails miserably, and they understand that they've lost touch with the market. Or their realization is incremental. For instance, Molly had created a profitable retailing web site and had run it successfully for five years, but in the sixth year she made a couple of relatively minor mistakes. She made a bad judgment call on a new hire, and she failed to keep up with a technological development that her competitor capitalized on. Molly would never have made these errors in the past, and she knew that she was no longer as engaged with her work as CEO as she should have been; she also knew that she was likely to have other lapses with much more serious consequences if she continued in her role. The likelihood of making more serious mistakes in the future convinced her that she was no longer the best person to be CEO and that she needed to move up to chairman; she decided to bring in someone who possessed the acumen and engagement necessary to do a good job.

Some entrepreneurs depart not because they're doing a bad job running the company but because they've lost their enthusiasm for it. There are plenty of serial entrepreneurs out there who love creating and building a company so that it's successful, but they aren't particular happy running a stable, profitable business. They know when they've reached the point when the company is finally doing well and more in need of a strong manager than a risk-taking innovator.

Agile entrepreneurs are always asking themselves two questions: Have I lost my passion for this business? and Have I lost my ability to lead and manage the business as well as I once did? If the answer to either question is yes, they then assess what their best role is if they step aside: as a big-picture strategist and spokesperson (i.e., chairman); as more of a leader than a manager (bringing in a COO); or removed entirely from the organization (either retaining a financial interest or selling his or her share of the company).

Entrepreneurs possess healthy egos, so it's sometimes difficult for them to consider leaving or taking on a lesser role in a company they built. Typically, they assume that the time will never arrive when it's ripe for a change. Here's a story that is a good reminder you can't assume you'll always be the best person for your job.

Tim, a departing CEO, held an exit interview with his successor, Martha, and during their discussion he explained that he had placed three important letters in his desk drawer, just as his predecessor had done for him. Tim explained that the letters were numbered and Martha should open them in order whenever a serious event took place and she needed help.

After a few months, the company encountered its first crisis during Martha's tenure. Its computer system broke down and caused a delay in shipping orders to customers. Encountering a barrage of complaints and criticism, Martha opened the desk drawer and letter number one, on which was written: "Blame it on your predecessor." Martha did what the letter suggested and remarkably was able to get through the crisis unscathed.

Then later that year, a second crisis occurred. Revenues dropped along with a corresponding decrease in productivity. Martha ran over to the desk drawer, found the second letter, and read, "Reorganize." She did as instructed and was rewarded with an uptick in productivity and revenues.

The next year, a third crisis occurred, even more serious than the rest. A bribery scandal involving overseas officials had created a big, negative media buzz. Martha, though, was not worried. She went over to the desk, opened the drawer, and read the third letter, which offered this advice: "Write three letters."

PUTTING CONCEPTS INTO ACTION

You may be one of the lucky ones who, besides being a brilliant business-starter, fund-raiser, and idea-generator, also leads and manages with great agility. Most entrepreneurs are more likely to be the former rather than the latter. And even those who are good leaders and managers may neglect developing their capacities in these areas because they're so consumed by other business issues. Most of you will benefit by making a concerted effort to expand your agility as a leader and a manager. To help you do so, answer the following questions related to key topics in the chapter:

Managerial Creativity

☐ Do you take the time to research a problem you're facing? Do you ask a lot of questions to help yourself develop options as a decision maker?

☐ Do you make a regular effort to involve others in your decisions, from direct reports to outside advisers?

☐ Are you able to articulate ideal objectives for a project, not only for yourself but for others? Does this ideal stimulate fresh thinking and unexpected approaches?

☐ How often do you have great conversations with your people, whether in person or via phone or electronically? Do these dialogues help you and others come up with creative solutions?

❑ Are you able to call a time-out when you and your team hit a wall? Can you step away from an issue and give yourself and others a creative break?

❑ Are you managing with too much or too little knowledge/involvement?

❑ Do you tend to focus your efforts only on areas you are skilled at or enjoy? Do you also tend to ignore managing those other areas or manage them perfunctorily?

❑ Are you reluctant to take advice or seek help in areas that you feel are your strengths? Do you give orders to others on these projects rather than ask questions and seek other perspectives?

Best Practices

❑ Do you feel that you're a motivational leader? Do you make a regular effort to generate excitement around a project and give people a reason to work harder or more innovatively?

❑ When you feel burned out or like you're just going through the motions, can you find a way to restore your energy? Do you have a method of re-energizing yourself as a leader, from taking a vacation to involving yourself in volunteer work, to pursuing a hobby?

❑ How much effort do you put into rewarding and recognizing your high-performers? Have you come up with different tactics to communicate how a given individual has made a difference in the company? Have you given this person rewards that are linked to his or her achievements?

❑ Are you willing to coach your people? Do you make the

effort to provide them with a sympathetic ear and wise counsel rather than just telling them what they need to do?

Developing and Running a Team

❑ Can you select team members based on their diversity and their complementary strengths, or do you tend to choose your favorites or people who share your ideas to be on key teams?

❑ How well do you handle team conflicts? Are you likely to forbid these conflicts or attempt to stifle them when they emerge, or are you able to manage them so that they often produce fresh ideas and bold new strategies?

Replacing Yourself

❑ Are you conscious of your performance as a manager and a leader and when that performance starts to decline, or do you believe that as the founder of the company and as the person who helped it succeed, you'll always be the best person to lead it?

❑ Have you ever stepped sideways or out in a company that you created? Did you do so because you recognized that you were no longer the best person for the stage to which the company had evolved?

❑ If you found that your company needed someone else to take over as its CEO, would you promote yourself to chairman and let someone else handle the day-to-day operational duties, or would you be willing to divest yourself entirely if you determined you were more hindrance than help to the company?

CHAPTER 10

Stretching Toward the Future

Change demands agility, and in the coming years we're going to witness an ever-increasing rate of change in all sectors of society. Google and other companies are already testing driverless cars that can be programmed to take people where they want to go. Nanotechnology, the process of manipulating the smallest molecular structures to create innovative new products, is making great progress in labs around the world. Global competition is reshaping the business landscape as India, Brazil, China, and other countries become dominant players in different industries. Global warming, health-care breakthroughs, and advances in social media are making status quo products and policies irrelevant.

As critical as agility is for entrepreneurs today, it will be even more critical in the future. Change has always created both great opportunities and obstacles for entrepreneurs, so it's logical to expect that as change becomes more pervasive and significant, opportunities and obstacles will increase as well.

This is true for all organizations, not just entrepreneurs, but the latter will feel the impact more, and they'll have more chances to take advantage of it. Large, public companies are protected to some extent by their size and resources; they can weather storms of change easier than entrepreneurs. By the same token, they are slower and less creative in their response, so entrepreneurs have a decided edge in this area.

A number of trends have already started that will soon gather steam and present entrepreneurs with opportunities and obstacles. We'll examine these trends and three other developments that will have a profound effect on entrepreneurial agility: innovation, collaboration, and information. First, though, we need to look at how entrepreneurial agility will facilitate capitalizing on trend-generated opportunities and overcoming obstacles.

TRACKING FOUR KEY TRENDS

I don't have a crystal ball, but I do have a great deal of experience in the technology and science sectors, and I feel comfortable making some forecasts about what we can expect in the next five or ten years. My goal here isn't to demonstrate my perspicacity— any reasonably astute observer of these fields probably could come up with similarly credible predictions—but to make the case that opportunities and obstacles will surface and that flexibility is crucial for dealing with both.

Continued Changes in Health Care

Obamacare is just the beginning. Invariably, it will evolve in unexpected ways, but we can be certain that reimbursement for services and products will become more tightly regulated. While large pharmaceutical companies and medical groups still dominate, this is likely to change. For one thing, we're seeing many of these companies reduce their research budgets. For another, a number of major patents are due to expire in the next five years, and this will result in more competition from lower-cost generic products. Similarly, we're seeing the rise of genetic tests to predict the best course of treatment for a patient with the least number of complications. In fact, gene replacement may be the wave of the future. We're already seeing studies linking nutrition to effects on genes, and it is logical to assume that using nutrition to deal with genetic issues will be a highly profitable field.

Entrepreneurs willing to take risks and enter new fields may be better able to compete against much larger companies. It takes agility to stretch outside of your comfort zone and take these actions. If you've never competed against a Fortune 500 company, for instance, you may be wary of introducing a low-cost generic drug and challenging a company with an expiring patent. At the same time, these are virgin opportunities, and the dramatic changes in health care invite the participation of risk-taking, innovative players and entrepreneurs who are adept at taking chances and being creative. Many such individuals are determining where they want to place new bets; this is how startup companies emerge from simple ideas and grow.

The Growing Need for Better Electronic Security

Target, American Express, and many other companies have been hit by online security breaches. As retailing and other financial transactions become increasingly digital, we're going to see a corresponding rise in thievery. Similarly, hackers are going to create more disruptive electronic viruses just because they can. It's not just huge companies who will be the victims of this malicious and illegal behavior but smaller organizations as well

Obviously, entrepreneurs whose businesses are built around selling security software based on rapidly aging technology are going to face serious obstacles. They will need to adopt the emerging technologies if they want to survive. At the same time, agile entrepreneurs who can create and market anti-virus software and establish more secure sites will enjoy a booming business. However, they'll need to shift their thinking so they are one step ahead of the hackers and criminals who are developing new wrinkles in their strategies to defraud and discombobulate. This means not marketing the same old virus protection software and methods but, rather, creating new and better virus fighters continuously. I've seen some companies hire brilliant hackers upon their release from prison and use their expertise to stretch their own development capabilities. This type of agility will be rewarded and is needed in this arena.

The Need for Better Methods of Crop Modification

The food business has always drawn more than its fair share of entrepreneurs, but the industry is changing rapidly for a variety of reasons, including the need for better methods of crop modification to increase resistance to drought and disease. This is an especially important requirement in Third World nations vulnerable to devastating weather events and food shortages. At the same time, there is growing concern about the negative impact of crop modification on health; the non-GMO movement has spread and real concern exists about the negative environmental impact of techniques designed to increase crop resistance to disease.

Entrepreneurs who stubbornly ignore these trends will suffer; these issues are not going away and probably will become even more significant in the coming years. Agile entrepreneurs, however, will view the trends as catalysts for changing products, services, and how and where they market them. Finding healthful crop modification methods is an ambitious goal, and it is one that will be achieved by entrepreneurial as well as large companies that test new approaches and employ innovative scientific researchers.

Nanotechnology

Nanotechnology and other innovative methods are reducing the size of electronics but increasing their power. Google Glass, a computer monitor that fits on the edge of eyeglasses, is just one example of this trend. In development are nanoparticles capable of delivering drugs more effectively than any other method. Increasingly smaller car batteries are evolving in labs and will soon replace the larger, more cumbersome batteries now in use.

The potential uses of nanotechnology are wide-ranging, and entrepreneurs with vision and creativity will be developing profitable products based on this technology in the coming years. The opportunity is there for agile entrepreneurs with the agility to think small rather than big, while more rigid small businesses that specialize in building large products will run into obstacles as their market gravitates toward nano-based products.

ADAPTING TO MIND-BOGGLING INNOVATIONS

Some people can't imagine cars that drive themselves, lunar vacations, and pills that protect people from forms of cancer,

Alzheimer's, and other diseases. Yet being open to hard-to-believe concepts will be a hallmark of agile entrepreneurs in the future. From my small corner of the science and technology universe, I've glimpsed various research and beta tests that are mind-boggling. Invariably, some of this work will spawn breakthrough products that will not only be incredibly profitable but also have the potential to reshape entire industries.

It's easy to dismiss these possibilities, though, because as creative and open-minded as entrepreneurs can be, they can also be close-minded when it comes to discoveries or experiments that threaten their businesses or the conventional wisdom. They've built companies with a certain set of assumptions as their foundation, and when some scientist in a lab renders those assumptions questionable by his work, they refuse to give that work credence. No one likes to consider that he may have to change his business based on new information, but this will be a way of life in the future. Advances in every field are coming at a rapid pace, and entrepreneurs willing to recognize the ones that are meaningful and respond by adapting their companies to cutting-edge knowledge will benefit enormously.

Gene sequencing, for instance, has become a much lower-cost process than in the past. It's widely predicted that at some point soon, a gene test on a silicon chip will become a common diagnostic for certain cancers. The ability to deliver key disease-treating genes to patients has progressed. All this means that some established methodologies for treating diseases will quickly become outmoded and new approaches will become the standard. Health-care entrepreneurs who recognize that this genetic research is game-changing will adapt to the emerging norm and be positioned to take advantage of this new standard.

A very different but related innovation involves silkworm "factories" where fibers are made that are stronger than steel. Genetic modification techniques have made this new, stronger fiber possible, and the implications for the fabric industry are significant. At some point, companies will be able to take advantage of silkworm technology and create more durable, longer-lasting products. Companies that are invested in old, durable materials will likely have to transition to this new fiber, and therein lies the obstacles and opportunities. Agile entrepreneurs who develop the capacity to supply this new fiber or adapt it for use in clothing, automobile car seats, and in other industries will benefit. However, it requires understanding a completely new technology and making the transition to its requirements.

Predictive analytics is a field that is bound to grow by leaps and bounds. Think about how a variety of businesses might change if we become more proficient at predicting the weather, trends in fashion, and the fads that will fade, as well as the ones that take hold. As we develop even better computers and software and we evolve our methods of collecting and analyzing data, we will become better able to predict everything from the path bad weather will take to the direction of the economy. Certainly opportunities exist for entrepreneurs who develop the best predictive models, but many more opportunities exist for small companies that figure out the best ways to use predictive analysis, either for their own businesses or as consultants to other businesses.

I've limited the discussion to three very diverse, mind-boggling innovations to give you a sense of the radical changes in the offing. I also ask you to consider how you might react to a radical innovation that affects your own business. I've found that rigid entrepreneurs react very differently from agile ones, that the former feel threatened by these changes while the latter are open-minded about them and explore their implications. It's not that every mind-boggling invention or event will pan out—some will seem huge at the beginning but then fizzle, while others may seem minor when an announcement is first made but they gain traction as very smart people develop the initial concept.

It's wise to monitor your own reaction to news of innovative developments that might require you to rethink aspects of your business. To help you monitor these reactions, here is a list of the common statements rigid and agile entrepreneurs make upon hearing about these developments:

The Rigid Entrepreneur

➤ The technology costs too much; no one will be able to afford it.

➤ Sure it looks promising, but they won't be able to turn it into something useable for years.

➤ I've seen these breakthroughs come and go; they never amount to anything.

The Agile Entrepreneur

➤ It looks like science fiction, but we need to monitor where the researchers take their discovery to see if it turns into anything that might be relevant to us.

➤ I think we need to invite these scientists to our next trade show so they can share what they're doing with people in our field.

➤ We've got to start doing our own research to see if we can apply what they've learned to our business.

MOVING FROM RUGGED INDIVIDUALISM TO COLLABORATIVE MINDSET

As I've emphasized, and as you probably know, entrepreneurs often like to go it alone. They prefer to create closed systems where they and their employees can work as an independent team to achieve their goals. At the extreme, some entrepreneurs adopt an underdog mentality and like to view themselves as a David succeeding amid organizational Goliaths. In other instances, small business owners can be insular, preferring the unilateral control that comes from operating without outside assistance.

This mindset has changed somewhat as opportunities have arisen in recent years that can't be capitalized on without some degree of collaboration. For example, some entrepreneurs are willing to give a stake in their company to an outside entity in exchange for financing or other resources that they lack internally and that they need to capitalize on an opportunity. Owing to the Internet and other digital media, it's now far easier for entrepreneurs to collaborate; social media bring various businesses together in different types of forums and electronic connectivity makes it simpler for collaborative groups to communicate with each other.

In the future, however, collaboration is not just going to be an option but a necessity. In Michael Leavitt and Rich McKeown's book *Finding Allies, Building Alliances*, the authors posit that a variety of social, economic, and technological forces will make collaboration an essential business tool in the near future. Leavitt, formerly governor of Utah and a Cabinet member under President George W. Bush, suggests that now, and especially in the next decade, small, agile networks will trump huge, rigid organizations; that the former will possess the diversity and speed that will confer a competitive edge that more homogeneous, slower entities can't match, no matter how big they are.

Entrepreneurs need to open themselves up to all the collaborative ventures that may emerge in the coming years. Here are some of the most promising ventures that already exist and are bound to become more numerous:

➤ **University Partnerships.** I've discussed this option earlier in the book, noting that universities are increasingly looking for entrepreneurial companies who can monetize the research of their academicians. In the future, these partnerships are likely to expand as traditional research-oriented universities face greater competition from the more practitioner-oriented online schools like Phoenix and Western Governors Universities. Combined with rising overhead (professor salaries, upgrading physical facilities), these academic-and-research-oriented institutions will be more eager than ever to find additional sources of income. Entrepreneurs who can establish strong relationships with research and technology directors at large universities can explore a variety of product possibilities and expect to have a more receptive partner than in the past, when some schools worried about the ethics of commercializing scholarly institutions.

➤ **Information Networks.** In the Leavitt-McKeown book on collaboration, they reference the Global Earth Observation System of Systems (GEOSS), an alliance of fifty-five countries designed to monitor environmental events, trends, and developments. The system is designed to promote free exchange of information across traditional and sometimes hostile boundaries. Invariably, we're going to see more data exchanges across boundaries in the commercial sector as technologies improve and make these exchanges feasible. It's not difficult to imagine a time when all entrepreneurs in a given industry set up an information exchange for use by all members to gain access to cutting-edge facts and figures relevant to their business. It's also possible that these networks will more closely resemble social networks but consist of a diverse user base—entrepreneurs in various fields who will share research, ideas, and data.

➤ **Professional Services Alliances.** Outsourcing has been a trend for years in large organizations, but entrepreneurs often like keeping all or most of their key employees in-house. I'm seeing a trend away from this policy, though, as the costs of providing health insurance and other employee benefits skyrocket and as highly competent professionals are downsized out of their corporate firms and are eager to partner with smaller companies. Agile entrepreneurs will take advantage of this trend and be willing to offer equity payments in exchange for high-quality consulting and services. Startups, especially, will take advantage of the availability of these top professionals at a time when they have little spare cash for salaries but a great need for expertise.

➤ **Big Company/Small Company Joint Ventures.** This type of collaborative effort is related to the previous one. Big organizations are relying on outsourced help in part because they've downsized to the point that they lack all the internal expertise they require; they have no choice but to go outside for assistance. Corporations may need an entrepreneurial group's expertise in anything from product development to information technology to accounting. In turn, entrepreneurs may require the funding or clout that a big company possesses.

The pace of big corporation/entrepreneur collaboration is bound to accelerate, in part because innovation has become the Holy Grail in executive suites, and entrepreneurs are nothing if not innovative. At the same time, the most innovative entrepreneurs will struggle to compete globally, and that's where a partnership with a big company can benefit them. Admittedly, some entrepreneurs are loath to form an alliance with a huge, global company—they hate dealing with bureaucracy. But with sufficient agility, entrepreneurs will figure out ways to cut red tape to achieve mutual objectives, and they'll convince their bigger partners to be similarly flexible in dealing with small operations who are unwilling to fill out forms in triplicate.

BECOMING AN INFORMATION MAGNET

Most entrepreneurs have trusted sources of information—their direct reports, their consultants, their attorneys, and so on. They rely on these sources to keep them up to date about technological developments, new laws that impact their businesses, and many other events and trends. Typically, they meet with a consultant monthly or schedule regular meetings with direct reports to go over new trends and developments. While entrepreneurs value the information they obtain from these sources, they tend to fall into information-obtaining ruts. Their sources are often homogeneous or even singular, and usually aren't particularly creative in their approach to information gathering.

While pundits have been talking about the "information revolution" for years, the real revolution is just around the bend. Increasingly, websites are combining with social media to offer users superior forms of information; accessing online communities of experts is becoming easier to do no matter what type of field you're in or expert you're searching for. Perhaps even more important, the global stew of information is being served up regularly on various sites; fascinating developments and discoveries are popping up from Western countries, as well as from places like India, China, Brazil, and elsewhere. Perhaps most significantly, the modes of electronic expression—be they tweets, posts, video blogs, etc.—are multiplying. Inevitably, these modes will continue to diversify and also become more user-friendly and impactful.

As a result of all these developments, entrepreneurs must start tapping more information sources more often if they expect to remain competitive. They must also be more innovative in their information-gathering strategies. They need to take advantage of Big Data and start pursuing ideas and facts as they emerge online through the use of analytics. If you want to see the future, visit the offices of Chicago-based global public relations firm Golin Harris. When you walk through their offices, you'll see a large section in which scores of young people sit in front of multiple monitors that give them access to a variety of social media, websites, television shows, and other forms of communication. They scour these monitors for news that might affect their clients and engage in conversation in various communities to gain perspective on this news. The look of this office is less like a traditional public relations firm and more like the flight deck of the Starship Enterprise.

To approach information in this manner requires agility. It means making a conscious effort to seek ideas and data from a more diverse group of people and organizations than in the past; it means being more active than passive in finding fresh opinions and provocative perspectives; and it means making this effort much more frequently. Here are some suggestions for how you might achieve these objectives:

➤ **Do digital customer analytics.** Big Data is more than a fact of business life; it's going to be an increasingly integral component of how all companies conduct business. Tech professionals are becoming much more astute in how they crunch the numbers they obtain from social media and other digital sites. They are able to gain great insight into customers' wants and needs, and this data can be used to communicate with them more effectively. In the next few years, tools to do analytics will be more widely available and easier for entrepreneurs to use.

➤ **Enter into online dialogues with community members.** Entrepreneurs thrive on fresh information and ideas, and online communities offer a chance to receive input that they might not get anywhere else. Being open to sharing information with people they don't know personally may be a challenge for some entrepreneurs, but this is where agility comes in. Stretching out of your comfort zone so you can dialogue with a professor in a science-based community might clue you in on the latest research that affects your product category. Another community member might give you a head's up about legislation being introduced that will have an impact on your efforts to sell to foreign markets.

➤ **Attend a more diverse group of seminars, workshops, and conferences.** As one entrepreneur told me when I asked him why he wasn't attending an industry conference, "Every day I'm away from the office is a day that I can't make money for the company." Entrepreneurs, much more so than larger organizational employees, view these types of activities as peripheral to their business. This is understandable, in that entrepreneurs succeed in large part because they devote great time and energy at the activities that benefit their companies the most. But as every business becomes more global, more digital, and more dependent on innovation, the need to stay current in order to stay competitive grows. It's critical that you expand your learning opportunities, which means seeking out the ever-expanding list of seminars, workshops, and conferences that affect your business and industry.

➤ **Make your own company a learning center.** Large organizations have created in-house "universities" to train and educate their employees, and entrepreneurs can do the same thing, albeit on a much smaller and less expensive scale. To increase the knowledge capacity of your staff, hold a roundtable focusing on a key industry trend. Invite experts to discuss and debate the subject and encourage your people to attend and participate. An even easier option is to schedule "speaker days" in which you find relevant business subject-matter experts (in manufacturing, customer service, information technology, etc.) or experts with broader business perspectives and have them deliver talks. Entrepreneurial companies tend to be insular, and the fast pace of change makes it difficult for successful companies to operate in relative knowledge isolation. If you are able to expand the knowledge base of your people through in-house educational tools, you can fight against this isolation.

➤ **Introduce iconoclasts, futurists, and other thought-catalysts into the business mix.** Fresh and sometimes divergent thinking will be essential in the coming years, in large part because traditional approaches won't be effective given the rise of unexpected challenges and opportunities. Due to game-changing developments in technology, competition from new global players, environmental restrictions that will impact most companies, and the evolving digital marketplace, entrepreneurs are going to have to vary their approaches. They may have to get rid of a customer service methodology that they've relied on for years or a product formulation that has served them well. To replace what is no longer effective, they'll need access to provocative concepts. They need to explore what is possible—and what may have seemed impossible a short time ago. In this way, they can consider alternatives that may lead to more effective strategies and tactics, products and policies.

PUTTING CONCEPTS INTO ACTION

How prepared are you for the future? It's difficult to prepare for tomorrow, let alone the next five years, when you're dealing with one crisis after the next or trying to gather the resources to go after a great opportunity before your competitors do. Agile entrepreneurs, however, develop a knack for dealing with present issues while also keeping one eye trained on the future.

To help you do the same, consider the following questions and how you might respond to them:

Tracking Trends

- ❑ Do you make an effort to be aware of events or developments in technology that might help or hamper your business?

- ❑ Do you monitor the legal, economic, health, and science fields for stories or announcements that may have long-term implications for your products and services?

- ❑ Do you talk about these trends with your people and discuss options if the trends gain steam and produce changes in your industry?

Focusing on Innovations

- ❑ Are you aware of the cutting-edge research taking place in universities, labs, and elsewhere that has the potential to reshape your business?

- ❑ Have you undertaken scenario planning that creates potential responses to these major innovations? Are you prepared to implement a plan that will shield you or take advantage of the situations that these innovations may produce?

❑ Are you more likely to dismiss innovative concepts
   or tests as unfeasible or begin discussion and planning
   in case they become feasible?

Becoming Collaborative

❑ How would you rate your current ability to partner
   with external organizations and institutions? Have you
   forged many or any alliances in the last few years with
   vendors, competitors, universities, or other groups?

❑ Do you actively seek partnering opportunities with
   large organizations? Are you ready, willing, and able
   to seek out these collaborations or are you reluctant
   to do so?

❑ Given where your company is weakest, might a
   partnership with an outside enterprise help you
   strengthen that weakness? Will strengthening it
   likely be even more important in the future
   than it is today?

Gathering Information

❑ Do you believe that your company has access to
   diverse and timely sources of information that have
   a direct bearing on your business? If the amount of
   this information were to double in the next five years,
   do you still believe you are prepared to access it
   effectively?

❑ Do you actively solicit ideas and data from a variety
   of external sources? Do you make a concerted,
   consistent effort to tap the minds of leading experts
   in your field, both in person and online?

❏ Are you open to business thinking that might be different from your own? Are you trying to develop a broad base of knowledge so that you're prepared to capitalize on new best business practices, policies, and processes?

Reflecting on these questions will help you become aware of your ability to be an agile entrepreneur as events unfold in the next few years. Even better, your responses may motivate you to be more flexible in your approach to innovation, information, trends, and collaboration, and to develop your capacity to learn and change as evolving situations dictate.

The future belongs to the nimble. I've tried to suggest all the different events and developments that will demand entrepreneurial agility, but I've only scratched the surface. Earlier in the book I advised you to "expect the unexpected," and that's doubly true advice for the next decade. We live in volatile, unpredictable times, and they're only going to become more volatile and unpredictable. Think about how much the business world has changed in the last ten years. Smartphones, mobile apps, and social media alone have created huge challenges for just about every company. More technological advances mixed with the growth of China and India as major players in the global marketplace combined with growing environmental concerns and consciousness will play havoc with every organization's best-laid plans.

Entrepreneurs, though, have an advantage over their larger business brethren moving forward. They possess a greater capacity for agility. Even though some entrepreneurs can become rigid in their attitudes and actions, they are inherently more flexible. They are not usually bound by stultifying bureaucracy, unyielding structures, or hidebound traditions. They are smaller, more innovative, and better able to maneuver as situations change.

I urge you to take advantage of this capacity for agility. In the next few years, you're bound to be surprised by events that neither I nor anyone else can predict. Don't react by becoming conservative, indecisive, risk-avoidant, status-quo focused, or insular. Instead, embrace out-of-the-box thinking, explore alternatives, seek a diversity of ideas and information, and test new approaches.

In this way, you'll set yourself and your business on an agile course that will help you deal with surprises and setbacks and pounce on opportunities before your competitors. Think and act agile, and you'll become the quintessential twenty-first century entrepreneur.

Index

2/15-0
1117 H